Boost Your Hiring IQ

Boost Your Hiring IQ

Carole Martin

McGraw-Hill
New York   Chicago   San Francisco
Lisbon   London   Madrid   Mexico City
Milan   New Delhi   San Juan   Seoul
Singapore   Sydney   Toronto

Copyright © 2007 by Carole Martin. All rights reserved. Printed in the United States of America. Except as permitted under the United States Copyright Act of 1976, no part of this publication may be reproduced or distributed in any form or by any means, or stored in a data base or retrieval system, without prior written permission of the publisher.

1 2 3 4 5 6 7 8 9 0   FGR/FGR   0 9 8 7

ISBN-13: 978-0-07-147701-7
ISBN-10: 0-07-147701-2

This publication is designed to provide accurate and authoritative information in regard to the subject matter covered. It is sold with the understanding that the publisher is not engaged in rendering legal, accounting, or other professional service. If legal advice or other expert assistance is required, the services of a competent professional person should be sought.
—*From a Declaration of Principles Jointly Adopted by a Committee of the American Bar Association and a Committee of Publishers and Associations*

McGraw-Hill books are available at special discounts to use as premiums and sales promotions, or for use in corporate training programs. For more information, please write to the Director of Special Sales, Professional Publishing, McGraw-Hill, Two Penn Plaza, New York, NY 10121-2298. Or contact your local bookstore.

This book is printed on acid-free paper.

Library of Congress Cataloging-in-Publication Data

Martin, Carole (Carole Hurd)
  Boost your hiring IQ / by Carole Martin.
    p. cm.
  Includes index.
  ISBN 0-07-147701-2 (alk. paper)
  1. Employee selection. I. Title.
HF5549.5.S38M37 2007
658.3′112—dc22
                              2006036393

Dad, this one's for you!

Contents

Acknowledgments

My sincere gratitude to my faithful editor, Donya Dickerson, who keeps me on my toes and inspires me to keep going and then picks up the pieces and puts them together.

Thank you to all the people who I have interviewed or have been interviewed by—and who have taught me what *not* to do as well as what *to do*.

Thanks to Milana Leshinsky and Kathy Sparks—my faithful teammates.

Thanks to my son, Stan Hurd, for his creativity and patience with his Mother.

Foreword

It just wasn't fair.

As the Interview Coach on Monster.com for the past 8 years, Carole Martin helped millions of job seekers deliver a polished and winning performance in their job interviews. As editor-in-chief of Monster.com, I saw Carole's advice transform even the most nervous entry-level beginner into a confident interviewer. Job seekers learned from Carole how to prepare for an interview, how to dress, how to listen, and how to win the job.

This was a great benefit to experienced managers, who knew that the best job interviews are conversations, not interrogations. Good interviewers got better results when they talked to job seekers who had studied Carole's advice.

Unfortunately, most hiring managers are not experts in the art of interviewing a candidate. When a "Martinized" candidate appeared in their offices, those interviews must have felt like amateurs by comparison. I'm sure that in the end they were rewarded with a better hire. But still: imagine their embarrassment!

Now, with *Boost Your Hiring IQ*, Carole has finally evened the playing field. In the first part of her book, she gives hiring managers a baseline score of how well they are doing at interviewing candidates. Then she describes clear and practical steps by which any hiring manager can boost his or her score quickly. It's an easy-to-follow template for interviewing success, one that hiring managers will return to again and again (especially those who never did get that degree in human resources while they were busy working for a living).

Building a great team in business takes clear thinking, a strong strategy, and an understanding of the big picture. All those factors are necessary and important, but if you can't assess candidates in the job interview, you're not going to put that understanding into practical application, day to day and year to year. There is no more important business decision—not one—than who to hire. Carole's book will give you the skills to hire right.

Doug Hardy,
coauthor with Jeff Taylor
of the Monster Careers *series*

Introduction

A Savvy Approach to More Effective Interviewing

I've heard it said that the only thing more painful than going to an interview is to have to conduct an interview. Most hiring managers dread the experience.

One of the reasons that they dread the experience is that they have had little or no training in how to effectively perform the task. There have been studies that have found that many hiring decisions are actually made in the first two minutes of the interview. If that is the case, these decisions are being made on a subjective basis, when the interviewers' inner prejudices are at work; they are judging the candidates by the way they look, act, shake hands, and most of all by their demeanor.

Most candidates are nervous before the interview. In fact, some are paralyzed at the thought of selling themselves. If the interviewer cannot see beyond that behavior and work to bring out the best in the person, the interviewer may be missing out on great people who are not great at interviewing or selling themselves.

Your job in the interview is to ask the questions that will bring out the skills, abilities, traits, and past behaviors of the candidate so that you can get as clear a picture of that person as a possible in a short amount of time.

Often hiring is done with little more than a passing thought to the skills, abilities, and knowledge needed for a position. Inadequate evaluation of critical skills costs companies millions of dollars each year because objective job data have not been collected.

As life has become more complicated, so has the interview-selection process. It appears that there is a competition going on as to who can be more effective at interviewing—the interviewer or the candidate.

Today's candidates are better prepared for the interview than candidates in the past, and they have practiced the difficult questions. Any bookstore or online career advice site has an assortment of books and help for the candidate to prepare for the encounter with the interviewer.

Just as interviewing for the job as a candidate is a learned skill, so is hiring a learned skill. The purpose of this book is to assist you in preparing for the interview.

Using the *Manager's Hiring IQ Test* to rate your interviewing skills will help you see where you need to strengthen your skills and your ability to ask more savvy questions. This fun and interactive quiz will also enable you to obtain more information from job candidates so that you will be able to determine objectively whether the person you're interviewing is the right person for the job.

This book is also intended to demonstrate to the interviewer the importance of listening for the *rehearsed* answer and how to probe for the *real* answer. The idea behind the book is to avoid costly hiring mistakes and to find the best qualified person for the job.

PART 1

The Manager's Hiring IQ Test

Benchmark Your Ability to Judge the Candidate

Whether you are a new interviewer or a professional who has extensive training, there is always room for improvement when it comes to selecting that right person for the job.

By predetermining key job factors for the job, you will identify the skills, abilities, and traits that you are seeking in a candidate.

The Manager's Hiring IQ Test in this part of the book examines your ability to ask the best questions possible so that you can obtain the best information possible from every question you ask. When you use the correct questions, you obtain information regarding patterns of behavior, and you begin to notice "red flags."

There are no incorrect answers in this hiring IQ test, but you will see that weak questions will lead you to a dead end with little information, while the stronger questions will allow you to go through more doors to gather the maximum information.

By being alert to red flags or negative patterns that candidates provide in their answers, you will begin to question and determine more about the person. You will begin to notice that there is more to interviewing than just listening to answers. You will be listening to what is *actually* being said, or what is *not* being said.

This Manager's Hiring IQ Test also introduces the idea of *probing* as a way to follow up on an answer and to dig deeper for more information. In other words, don't just stop with one question. You will want to dig deeper—using probing to find out as much as possible about the candidate's ability to do the job.

Regardless of how you score the first time, use the test by periodically taking it to see if you can *boost* your hiring IQ.

> By reading through the questions before you interview a candidate, you will become more comfortable and learn the strongest way to ask a question and get the most information possible in a short amount of time.

IQ Test Instructions

After every *interviewer's question* there are three possible questions to choose from: (A), (B), or (C). It is your task to select the strongest way for an interviewer to ask the question—*the one that will provide you with the most information.* Which answers provide an in-depth look at the candidates' skills and experiences, as well as his or her past behavior? For each question, determine which of the questions is more effective than the others.

- Which is the *strongest* question?

- Which is the *mediocre* question?

- Which is the *weakest* question?

After you finish taking the quiz, you can score yourself and rate your interviewing skills.

The Tests

There are 50 questions that have been divided into two categories. The first 25 are general questions, and the next 25 are behavioral questions. Take the tests and determine how you stand as an interviewer. What is your interview hiring IQ?

Test One: General Interview Questions (1–25)

General questions are broad in nature and can be used in almost any interview. The object with this type of question is to gain as much information about the candidate as possible.

As you listen to answers, listen for key words and patterns to each response. You may have to read between the lines by listening for clues to the candidate's abilities and trusting your intuition.

A good rule to follow before you interview a candidate is: *leave your judgment* at the door and bring your *intuition* into the room.

INTERVIEWER'S QUESTION

1. **Learning about a candidate's background and experience.**
   Select the strongest question—the one that will provide you with the most information.

   (A) Walk me through your résumé.

   (B) Tell me about yourself.

   (C) How would you describe yourself in three words?

   I think the strongest question is _____.

ANSWERS

The Strongest Question

(B) This question is the strongest because it is will often provide you with the most telling answer. It is an open-ended question that allows the candidate to say whatever he or she wants to focus on. Here is your chance to listen to where the candidate's information focuses. Is the answer succinct, or does it tend to ramble off in different directions?

Does the answer sound like something out of a book and rehearsed, or conversational and natural?

The information you obtain from the answer to this question will be a good source for probes now or later in the interview. If the candidate claims to have saved his or her last company money, you could probe by asking a question such as, "Tell me more about the time you saved the company money."

Ideally this answer should give you a good summary or image of the person you are interviewing. If not, that is a clue that the candidate is either not prepared or the candidate doesn't know what he or she can bring to the job. Your job is to probe for more information.

The Mediocre Question

(C) This is a mediocre question as it stands. It becomes stronger if you probe and ask for an example of the words used to describe the person. For example, if the candidate claims to be "organized," you can ask for an example of the last time he or she organized a complete project or event and how he or she logistically planned and organized the project.

The Weakest Question

(A) This is the weakest question because it is information you can get by reading through the résumé. There is little or no new information received from the answer. Résumé writers do a great job of putting out excellent résumés. If all a candidate has to do is walk you through the text, there is not much real information gained from the question.

RATE YOURSELF

If you chose question **(B),** give yourself 5 points.

If you chose question **(C)**, give yourself 3 points.

If you chose question **(A)**, give yourself 0 points. _____

INTERVIEWER'S QUESTION

2. **Determining what a candidate has to offer that the other candidates don't have.**
   Select the strongest question—the one that will provide you with the most information.

   (A) What makes you unique?

   (B) Why should I hire you?

   (C) What qualities do you have that the last candidate did not have?

   I think the strongest question is _____.

ANSWERS

The Strongest Question

(A) Although any of these questions could assist you in gaining valuable information, this question is the strongest because it asks for information that requires some original thought on the part of the candidate.

In the event that all the candidates you are interviewing for the position are equally qualified, you will be looking for a "tie-breaker" or some quality that will distinguish this person from the competition.

The Mediocre Question

(C) This question, like question (A), may catch the candidate off guard. What you are really asking is, "What are the strengths that you bring to this job?" But by asking the question and using more original wording, you may find that you get more information and thought from the candidate.

A bonus from this question is that you can determine what research the candidate has done and how familiar he or she is with the job description/posting.

The Weakest Question

(B) Somewhere there is a rule written that states, "You should never begin a question with the word *why*." The word *why* puts candidates on the defensive, and they feel they must defend themselves or withhold something from the interviewer because they feel they will be judged unfairly.

A better way to ask this question is: "What can you bring to this position that the other candidates cannot?"

RATE YOURSELF

If you chose question **(A)**, give yourself 5 points.

If you chose question **(C)**, give yourself 3 points.

If you chose question **(B)**, give yourself 0 points. _____

You should avoid beginning a question with the word *why*. It puts candidates on the defensive.

INTERVIEWER'S QUESTION

3. **Learning if a candidate has what it takes to do the job.**
    Select the strongest question—the one that will provide you with the most information.

    (A) How would you rate yourself as a fit for this job?

    (B) What do you see as the most important qualities needed to do this job?

    (C) What added value would you bring to this job?

    I think the strongest question is _____.

ANSWERS

The Strongest Question

(B) This is the strongest question because it can easily be followed up with a probe. The candidate might answer the question by saying something like, "I think the most important quality needed to do this job would be creative problem solving."

This provides you with the opportunity to find out how the candidate rates him or herself on creative problem solving. Depending on the answer given, you can ask for an example of a time when he or she used creative problem solving to think "outside the box."

The Mediocre Question

(C) This is an acceptable question because, like the strongest one, it may catch the candidate off guard by the way you ask it.

What you are really asking is, "What are the strengths that you bring to this job?" By asking the question using more original wording than the "strengths" question, you may get more thoughtful information from the candidate.

Candidates will also have to be prepared and have done their research about the job to know what is expected in this position and how their "added value" can bring even more than asked for in the posting or ad. So a bonus to this question is that the candidate's answer may let you know how familiar the candidate is with the position and your company.

The Weakest Question

(A) The question is itself is too closed and will reveal very little information of value unless the candidate offers it or you probe with a second question such as, "Could you tell me what areas of the job would be a good fit for you?" Or, you could ask, "Is there any aspect of the position where you feel you will have to stretch to come up to speed?"

RATE YOURSELF

If you chose question **(B)**, give yourself 5 points.

If you chose question **(C),** give yourself 3 points.

If you chose question **(A),** give yourself 0 points. _____

INTERVIEWER'S QUESTION

4. **Determining if you have a personality fit.**
   Select the strongest question—the one that will provide you with the most information.

   (A) How would you describe your relationship with your coworkers at your current job?

   (B) What kinds of people do you like working with?

   (C) List three things about your personality that will make me want to hire you.

   I think the strongest question is _____.

ANSWERS

The Strongest Question

(A) This is the strongest question because it asks for more than a single-word response. If candidates answer with a single word, that should be a *red flag* that they are not open communicators.

Turn up your listening skills to read between the lines if the answer seems too good to be true. Such an answer might be, "I get along with *everyone*." It is difficult to believe that a person can get along with *everyone*. In order to fully test this type of answer, be sure to follow up with a behavioral question such as, "Tell me about a time when you had a conflict or a difference of opinion with a coworker." You'll learn more about behavioral questions in Part 2.

The Mediocre Question

(C) This is a mediocre question because it can be answered with three words and nothing more, unless you probe for the reason behind the answer. A stronger way to ask this question would be to say, "Describe three personality traits that your coworkers would use to tell me about you."

If candidates answer with a single-word answer, they haven't listened to the question. They probably haven't thought about what their coworkers think about them. As with any single-word answer, you will need to obtain more information by probing with additional questions.

The Weakest Question

(B) This is the weakest question because it is too narrow in scope to provide you with much information. What if they say "smart people"? You will not have gained much information about the values and tolerance of this person. By asking a broader question such as, "What exposure have you had to working with people from diverse backgrounds and cultures?" you will be finding out how much work he or she has done in different environments. In today's global work environment you may want to look for people who are tolerant and accepting so that they can fit into a variety of situations with a variety of people and still be comfortable.

RATE YOURSELF

If you chose question **(A),** give yourself 5 points.

If you chose question **(C)**, give yourself 3 points.

If you chose question **(B)**, give yourself 0 points. _____

INTERVIEWER'S QUESTION

5. Determining a candidate's motivation.

Select the strongest question—the one that will provide you with the most information.

(A) When were you most satisfied in your job?

(B) Do you mind work that is somewhat routine and mundane?

(C) What was your most rewarding experience on your job?

I think the strongest question is _____.

ANSWERS

The Strongest Question

(A) This is the strongest question because if the candidates can tell you when they were most satisfied, you will know when they have been most motivated. People who are energized by their jobs are more motivated than those who are not. In turn these people are better performers and stay longer with the job and company. When people are bored or hate their job, their performance usually reflects their motivation. Therefore, if candidates were motivated in past jobs that are similar to the one you are trying to fill, it is likely that they will be motivated again.

The Mediocre Question

(C) This question is okay because it asks the candidates to think about their favorite job experience, and this could be very positive. If, however, the candidates cannot come up with an answer, perhaps they haven't had a rewarding experience. This is a red flag to watch for as an indication that this worker isn't really turned on by the job he or she is applying for. While not all people have to be excited about their work, contented employees make more motivated workers.

The Weakest Question

(B) This is the weakest question because it is closed-ended and can be answered with a simple yes or no. And, who would answer yes to being bored by routine or mundane work—even if they were? The question could be described as leading the candidate. It's akin to saying, "You wouldn't really mind if the work was not interesting, would you?" This question will provide you with little valuable information regarding the motivation of the candidate.

RATE YOURSELF

If you chose question **(A)**, give yourself 5 points.

If you chose question **(C)**, give yourself 3 points.

If you chose question **(B)**, give yourself 0 points. _____

INTERVIEWER'S QUESTION

6. **Learning about potential problems that could affect performance.**

   Select the strongest question—the one that will provide you with the most information.

   (A) Is there any reason that you will not be able to perform the duties of the job with reasonable accommodation?

   (B) Did you get any negative feedback from your last job?

   (C) Do you have any health problems that would keep you from doing the job?

   I think the strongest question is _____ .

ANSWERS

The Strongest Question

(A) This is the best way to ask this question. You are treading on sensitive ground when you begin to ask about limits or disabilities. Be sure to ask the question so that it is not discriminatory against people with disabilities.

The term "reasonable accommodation" is somewhat vague. Be aware that this question has the possibility of eventually coming back to haunt you if the candidate feels that you discriminated against him or her.

The Mediocre Question

(B) This question is just average because it is not specific enough to garner any information that might be helpful. A stronger way to ask this question would be, "Tell me about a comment on your last performance appraisal, or from your boss, that indicated you needed to improve in some area of your performance."

The Weakest Question

(C) This question is not only weak, but it is illegal to ask. The Americans with Disabilities Act states that you cannot ask questions regarding health unless health is relevant to the requirements of the job and the duties that will to be performed. You can ask if there are any reasons the candidate cannot perform the duties of the job with reasonable accommodation.

RATE YOURSELF

If you chose question **(A)**, give yourself 5 points.

If you chose question **(B)**, give yourself 3 points.

If you chose question **(C)**, give yourself 0 points. _____

INTERVIEWER'S QUESTION

7. **Learning about how a candidate gets along with others.**
   *Select the strongest question—the one that will provide you with
   the most information.*

   (A) How would your coworkers describe you?

   (B) Would you describe a time when you had a conflict with someone at work?"

   (C) Have you ever had a disagreement with a boss or coworker?

   I think the strongest question is _____.

ANSWERS

The Strongest Question

(B) This is the strongest question because it asks for a description of a behavior. The answer given will be an indicator of how candidates have acted in the past. You are not asking what they would do *if* they had a conflict with someone, but what they did *when* they had a conflict. If they say they've never had a conflict, further probing may be required to find out if this is a passive or weak person who may not stand up for himself.

This is not to say that all candidates must have a great conflict answer, but they should at least be able to describe situations in which there were differences of opinion and how they successfully resolved them.

The Mediocre Question

(A) This question is just average because the answer will only tell you how candidates think others view them as a person. It does not ask for specific information, such as "How would your coworkers describe your team spirit—or your effect on the team?

If they describe themselves as someone who "gets along with everyone," you should probe to find out if they do indeed get along with everyone. You could ask about a time when someone may have done something that the candidates disapproved or had a difference of opinion about, and how they handled the problem.

The Weakest Question

(C) It is difficult to believe that someone could work with other team members and be 100 percent amiable to all things, day in and day out. For this reason, this is the weakest question. If the candidate answered this question with a no answer, you will need to use the other questions given to get to the behavioral patterns of this person. Is he or she too passive or agreeable and not able to stand up for himself or herself?

RATE YOURSELF

If you chose question **(B),** give yourself 5 points.

If you chose question **(A),** give yourself 3 points.

If you chose question **(C),** give yourself 0 points. _____

INTERVIEWER'S QUESTION

8. **Understanding how candidates cope with failure.**
   Select the strongest question—the one that will provide you with the most information.

   (A) What has been your biggest career setback?

   (B) If you could go back in your career, what would you change?

   (C) Have you ever missed a deadline?

   I think the strongest question is _____.

ANSWERS

The Strongest Question

(A) This question will evoke a variety of answers—and for that reason it is the strongest. The greatest reward is sometimes the process of overcoming the problem and not the problem itself. Listen carefully to see what kind of determination this person demonstrates, especially after facing a problem. Listen to what he or she learned from the situation. You are seeking an answer that will show assertiveness and willpower, especially after facing adversity.

The Mediocre Question

(B) This is another "spin me a tale" question. It is a good question because it asks for some introspection and about lessons learned, but it's weak because it doesn't ask for specifics. You should listen to the tone of this answer and then for the attitude when the answer is given. Is it upbeat and positive or regretful and angry? You could probe deeper for more information about the lesson learned and how the lesson learned might be applied to the position you're seeking to fill.

The Weakest Question

(C) This is the weakest question because it is too broad and can be answered with a simple yes or no/ If the candidate does not expand on his or her answer, then it will be your job to probe deeper to find out about the particular event or events that led to a missed deadline. You will also want to find out if this was an isolated incident or something that happens often or periodically.

A stronger way to ask this question would be to ask, "Could you tell me about an incident that involved missing a deadline?" Now you have asked for a specific example of an incident involving a missed deadline.

RATE YOURSELF

If you chose question **(A)**, give yourself 5 points.

If you chose question **(B)**, give yourself 3 points.

If you chose question **(C)**, give yourself 0 points. _____

INTERVIEWER'S QUESTION

9. **Determining someone's ability to learn from mistakes.**
    Select the strongest question—the one that will provide you with the most information.

    (A) What is the most important lesson you learned in your work by making a mistake?

    (B) What would you do if you made a mistake and someone else was going to be blamed?

    (C) We all make mistakes. What was one of your most recent mistakes on the job?

    I think the strongest question is _____.

ANSWERS

The Strongest Question

(A) It is difficult for candidates to discuss failure in an interview when they are trying to sell themselves, but this question is the strongest because it asks for the positive, not the negative. It will be confident, assured candidates who can talk about lessons learned without feeling that they are in hot water when they answer this question in an interview. Listen carefully and try to read if the candidate really did learn a significant lesson from the experience.

The Mediocre Question

(C) This is an okay question because of the tone of the question as much as the question itself. As the interviewer, you have admitted that we all make mistakes. The candidate sees that you understand the situation and trusts you not to be judgmental about mistakes and as a result may respond more readily.

Candidates' answers may reveal whether or not they agree that it's okay to make mistakes and that life situations happen to everyone. What you will be listening for is the lessons learned or the attitude of self-forgiveness instead of self-deprecation.

The Weakest Question

(B) This is the weakest question because it doesn't ask for a specific example. When you ask, "What would you do if" questions, you are asking the candidates to make up a story. What you want is for them to show you proof of their work history.

The answer in this case may reveal as much about the person's integrity and loyalty as it would about the mistake itself. Not only must candidates deal with a mistake but also with the idea that they could get away with something at a cost to someone else.

RATE YOURSELF

If you chose question **(A)**, give yourself 5 points.

If you chose question **(C)**, give yourself 3 points.

If you chose question **(B)**, give yourself 0 points. _____

INTERVIEWER'S QUESTION

10. **Probing for something missing or hidden in the candidate's experience.**
    Select the strongest question—the one that will provide you with the most information.

    (A) Tell me something negative about yourself.

    (B) I am concerned about the gaps in your résumé. Can you explain them?

    (C) You seem to be overqualified for this job. What attracted you to this position?

    I think the strongest question is _____.

ANSWERS

The Strongest Question

(C) This is the strongest question because it is getting a concern on the table and allowing the candidates to give reasons for applying for a job that they may be overqualified for. It is worth listening for extenuating circumstances before you make a judgment.

Sometimes there are reasonable explanations for why the person has opted to "step down" or change careers—and you may get a real bargain in the process. Obviously, you will have to listen carefully to the answer and make a judgment about its authenticity before you can move forward. If you are concerned about the fact that the person will get bored and not stay in the job, you will need to probe deeper regarding future goals and plans.

The Mediocre Question

(B) This is an okay question because it addresses a legitimate concern that requires information. Where has this person been during the gaps? And are the gaps indicators that there is a pattern of on-again, off-again employment?

There may be very legitimate reasons why a candidate took time off. Be sensitive to women with gaps and not push in a negative manner when it comes to maternity leaves. The same would be true with medical leaves and your reaction to this information.

The Weakest Question

(A) This is the weakest question because it is not specific. It's actually a "trick" question that can work against both you and the candidate. Whatever the candidate answers will be a problem because the question has a negative slant.

RATE YOURSELF

If you chose question **(C),** give yourself 5 points.

If you chose question **(B)**, give yourself 3 points.

If you chose question **(A)**, give yourself 0 points. _____

INTERVIEWER'S QUESTION

11. **Determining which accomplishment the candidate is proudest of.**

    Select the strongest question—the one that will provide you with the most information.

    (A) Have you earned any rewards or received bonuses for a particular project?

    (B) List three of your accomplishments that you would like me to know about.

    (C) What is the work that you've been most proud of in all of your jobs?

    I think the strongest question is _____.

ANSWERS

The Strongest Question

(C) This is the strongest question because it emphasizes the achievement that has given the most satisfaction. In other words, it leads a candidate to discuss a project that was motivating. This question can bring forth information that you may not have otherwise gotten if you had asked the question in a different way. To make the question even stronger, it would be appropriate to ask for more details. You could ask, "Tell me about the things that you did that made the job the most satisfying."

The Mediocre Question

(B) This works only as long as you can probe for further details. The answer to this question should not only explain a specific project a candidate works on but it should also give some information as to his or her role in the project. If the information is not offered, then it is your job to ask for more details or a specific example:

- Could you tell me about some specific actions you took?

- What exactly was your role?

- Did you achieve your goal?

The Weakest Question

(A) This is the weakest way to find out this type of information because this question is too broad in scope: "Have you ever?" Also, it is too narrow a question to get useful information. There are jobs in certain companies that may never receive any rewards or kudos. And there are other companies that hand out rewards and kudos like candy. You will have to determine through probing whether or not this was an unusual event or a common occurrence.

RATE YOURSELF

If you chose question **(C),** give yourself 5 points.

If you chose question **(B),** give yourself 3 points.

If you chose question **(A),** give yourself 0 points. _____

INTERVIEWER'S QUESTION

12. Talking about the candidate's strengths.

Select the strongest question—the one that will provide you with the most information.

(A) If I asked your coworkers to describe your strengths, what would they tell me and why?

(B) What are your strengths?

(C) What can you offer this company?

I think the strongest question is _____.

ANSWERS

The Strongest Question

(A) This is the strongest question because it requires introspection from the candidate. Although it asks the basic question, "What are your strengths?" it has a new twist because you ask for the information through the words of others.

Does the answer focus on knowledge-based skills such as education or experience? Or are the words used focused more on transferable traits that can be used in any job? A few examples of transferable traits are communication, problem solving, time management, and organizational skills.

Or are the words used in the answer focused on character traits? These words would include shy, happy, easy-going, and good sense of humor. The best answer will have a combination of all types of traits. If that is not the case, it will be your job to ask about each category and what others would say about the candidate's different traits.

The Mediocre Question

(B) What makes this question mediocre is that it is very trite. Almost every book on interviewing includes this question as one of the top 10 interviewing questions. There are more creative ways of asking for the same information, such as: What is the strongest quality you could bring to this job?

The Weakest Question

(C) This question is very vague. "What can you bring?" The candidate will bring a number of things, but which is most relevant to this job? If you do ask this question, be specific:

- After reading the job description, where do you think you are the strongest match? Weakest match?

- When you compare this job with your past jobs, where are the similarities in the jobs you performed?

RATE YOURSELF

If you chose question **(A)**, give yourself 5 points.

If you chose question **(B)**, give yourself 3 points.

If you chose question **(C)**, give yourself 0 points. _____

INTERVIEWER'S QUESTION

13. **Learning about candidates' experience with working in teams and groups.**
   Select the strongest question—the one that will provide you with the most information.

   (A) Have you ever done anything to promote collaboration in a group?

   (B) What was the most rewarding experience you've had in motivating people?

   (C) Have you been on a team on which someone was not pulling his or her weight?

   I think the strongest question is _____.

ANSWERS

The Strongest Question

(B) This question asks specifically for the *most* rewarding experience. If you are seeking leadership qualities, this is the best question for finding out whether or not the person has ever motivated anyone.

If candidates do not respond with a specific answer, you can assume that they haven't motivated anyone or that they haven't thought about how motivating others is a part of teamwork and cooperation. If you are looking for a strong leader or cheerleader, you will need to probe further to find out what kind of a team player this person is and whether he or she will fit into your environment.

The Mediocre Question

(C) This is an okay question because it is a chance for you to listen for what this person does when there is a problem or conflict with the team. The skills that you would be listening for in the answer to this question are whether the candidate took the initiative and did anything about the problem.

Also, if the candidate was proactive, what approach did he or she take? Ideally this question would be answered with an example or story.

The Weakest Question

(A) Any question that can be answered with a single word, like this one, is a weak question. In addition, this question is confusing because of the word "anything." What exactly do you consider "anything"? The candidate may not understand where you are going with this question and may not run with the answer.

A much stronger question would be to ask candidates about their ability to make the team stronger by some particular action they took or idea they had. For example: Tell me about a time when you worked in a team environment and what role you played.

RATE YOURSELF

If you chose question **(B)**, give yourself 5 points.

If you chose question **(C)**, give yourself 3 points.

If you chose question **(A)**, give yourself 0 points. _____

INTERVIEWER'S QUESTION

14. Learning what the candidate's biggest challenge would be if he or she got this job.

Select the strongest question—the one that will provide you with the most information.

(A) How would you compare and contrast this job with your last job?

(B) What steps do you take when you are faced with a new situation or challenge?

(C) What do you foresee being the biggest challenge for you in this job?

I think the strongest question is _____.

ANSWERS

The Strongest Question

(A) This question is a great measure of what job skills someone is comfortable and familiar with and what is completely different from his or her previous experience.

By probing the candidates' areas of expertise, you can flush out their strengths based on what they've done in the past. If you hear something that is of particular importance and they performed that task in their last job, you will want to ask for a specific example of a time when they did that and the results they received.

The Mediocre Question

(C) This question is just okay because you are really asking about where the candidate is a weak fit for this particular job. Listen to how the candidate answers and observe his or her body language and comfort level when talking about something that is negative. Being challenged can be something the candidates could turn around if they are comfortable with the question, letting you know how they pick up things quickly and giving you an example of how they did so in past jobs.

Whether you are willing to accept the weakness will depend on what percentage of the job is affected by this lack of knowledge, and also what the other candidates bring to the job that this candidate may not.

The Weakest Question

(B) This is the weakest way to ask this question. A stronger approach would be to ask a question about past experience, such as, "What steps have you taken in the past when you've been faced with a new situation or challenge?"

By requesting specific details about their past actions, you are more likely to get an example that demonstrates how the candidates worked through difficult situations in the past.

RATE YOURSELF

If you chose question **(A),** give yourself 5 points.

If you chose question **(C),** give yourself 3 points.

If you chose question **(B),** give yourself 0 points. _____

INTERVIEWER'S QUESTION

15. Determining particular areas of expertise.

Select the strongest question—the one that will provide you with the most information.

(A) What are the areas of expertise that you believe you know better than anyone else?

(B) What is the strongest quality that you can bring to this position?

(C) How do you keep abreast of trends within your field of expertise?

I think the strongest question is _____.

ANSWERS

The Strongest Question

(A) This is the strongest question because it asks the candidates to explain what makes them more qualified than the other candidates. They can determine the job requirements from the job description. This area of expertise could be a "hard" skill or one that is considered to be a "soft" skill. The hard skills would encompass anything that is covered under education and experience. The softer skills, which are sometimes underestimated, are transferable skills and personal traits or qualities.

In other words, it is a good interview if you can find out enough about the candidate to decide whether this is the right person for the job. If you look only at the hard skills, you may later regret that you hadn't seen the red flags regarding transferable skills or personal traits.

The Mediocre Question

(C) To make this question work, you'd have to follow up by asking, "How current are you with the trends and improvements in this industry/field?" It is important to find out if the person is staying abreast of the latest trends and technology.

You should listen for any courses or training this person is planning to take or has taken to stay current. Another good way to stay abreast of the industry is through memberships in organizations. If you are knowledgeable about what is available to keep up with industry changes, you will be able to probe for more specific information to determine if the person is doing as much as possible to remain industry-savvy.

The Weakest Question

(B) This is the weakest question because it is essentially just another version of the question, "What are your strengths?" This question asks for the strongest quality, and you will need more information about that quality and whether it applies to the job you are interviewing for. You will do this by probing for a reason that the person has named that particular quality.

RATE YOURSELF

If you chose question **(A)**, give yourself 5 points.

If you chose question **(C)**, give yourself 3 points.

If you chose question **(B)**, give yourself 0 points. _____

INTERVIEWER'S QUESTION

16. Ascertaining the candidate's communication skills.

Select the strongest question—the one that will provide you with the most information.

(A) Rate your communication skills. Are they excellent, above average, or average?

(B) What percentage of your current job requires good communication skills, and how does that percentage fit with the rest of your job?

(C) How do you think your coworkers would describe your communication skills?

I think the strongest question is _____.

ANSWERS

The Strongest Question

(B) This is the strongest answer, particularly because it has two parts. The first part of the question—the percentage—could be answered with one word. When you add the second part of the question you are asking for a more specific answer. "How does that percentage fit into the rest of your position?" In other words, 40 percent of your job may require answering the phone in a professional manner. That may impress you until you find out that the phone is the only communication the candidate has with people beyond that 40 percent. This is acceptable provided your candidate does not need to have a broader range of communication skills. By adding the second part of the question, you will find out about the extent of the candidate's interface with others as a whole.

The Mediocre Question

(C) This is not the strongest question, but it does ask for a specific trait and is an excellent way to test how the candidate rates his or her skills through the lens of a group of peers. Speaking through others' words is much easier for some candidates and so they may be able to speak more freely than they would if they had to use their own words.

The Weakest Question

(A) With a question like this one, you will not gather any valuable information. It is unlikely that people are going to rate themselves average during the interview, even if they are. The candidate is there to impress and sell you. What decent salesperson would ever say that his or her product was average?

You can strengthen this question by asking a follow-up such as: Give me an example of a typical day in which you are using your communication skills.

RATE YOURSELF

If you chose question **(B)**, give yourself 5 points.

If you chose question **(C)**, give yourself 3 points.

If you chose question **(A)**, give yourself 0 points. _____

INTERVIEWER'S QUESTION

17. Determining candidates' attention to detail.

Select the strongest question—the one that will provide you with the most information.

(A) How are you at handling details?

(B) When it comes to detail, how would you rate yourself on a scale of 1 to 10?

(C) What types of details do you handle in your current job, and what types of details did you handle in previous jobs?"

I think the strongest question is _____.

ANSWERS

The Strongest Question

(C) This is the strongest way to ask the question because it allows the candidate to talk about former experiences. This question is open-ended and will flush out whether the candidate is prepared to discuss previous work and can do so in an articulate manner. This question also allows you to delve deeper into the kinds of details handled on previous jobs.

You can probe by adding such things as:

- Tell me more about your previous job and how you successfully handled detail.

- Give me an example of a project you worked on that required you to deal with a great amount of detail.

The Mediocre Question

(B) While quantifiers or numbers are a good way to measure information, this question is only a mediocre one to ask unless you probe into the reason the candidate chose a particular number as a rating.

For instance, if candidates assign themselves a 10, then you should ask what makes them a 10. The same is true if they were to say a 5, and you could follow up with a question such as, "What kept you from rating yourself a 10?" The answer to this will provide you with significant information about the candidate.

The Weakest Question

(A) It is unlikely that a candidate would say "bad" or "weak." If you get a single-word answer such as "good," "ok," or "excellent," then probe with the following follow-up questions:

- What makes you say "excellent"?

- Can you give me a specific example?

RATE YOURSELF

If you chose question **(C)**, give yourself 5 points.

If you chose question **(B)**, give yourself 3 points.

If you chose question **(A)**, give yourself 0 points. _____

INTERVIEWER'S QUESTION

18. Assessing the candidate's organizational skills.

Select the strongest question—the one that will provide you with the most information.

(A) How would you rate your organizational skills?

(B) If you had several projects at once, how would you decide the priorities?

(C) What would your last boss say about your ability to organize projects?

I think the strongest question is ____.

ANSWERS

The Strongest Question

(C) This is the best question because it asks for something that can be verified. If you were to check a candidate's references and ask the person's last boss about his or her ability to organize projects, you could verify whether the candidate gave accurate information.

Even if you don't check the reference, candidates may be concerned that you might. Chances are the candidates will be forthright because they may fear you will check out their claim.

The Mediocre Question

(B) This is a situational question that the candidate can answer with a make-believe scenario, thus making it less strong. Candidates could spin you a tale, saying something such as, "I would first . . . , and then I would . . . ," when they really haven't ever done such a thing before. Because it sounds good, it may be difficult to tell fact from fiction with this type of question. At the same time, it does demonstrate how the candidate thinks through the problem with limited information. If they solve the problem by asking the boss for help—this could be a "red flag."

The Weakest Question

(A) This is another of those questions that fails to glean much information. The person could give you a number or even a rating, but it doesn't give you anything to compare the answer to. If candidates give themselves a 10 rating, you will still have to determine what is being compared. The question would be stronger if, after you asked, "How would you rate your organizational skills?" you then asked a follow-up question such as, "Can you explain how you decided on that number for your rating?"

RATE YOURSELF

If you chose question **(C),** give yourself 5 points.

If you chose question **(B),** give yourself 3 points.

If you chose question **(A),** give yourself 0 points. _____

INTERVIEWER'S QUESTION

19. Rating someone's problem-solving skills.

Select the strongest question—the one that will provide you with the most information.

(A) What approach or steps do you take when you're faced with a problem?

(B) How much problem analysis did you do in your last position?

(C) Was there a time when you identified a significant problem in your past job?

I think the strongest question is _____.

ANSWERS

The Strongest Question

(C) This is the strongest question because it requests a specific time or incident when a problem occurred. There is always the chance that the candidate might give a yes or no answer. If the answer to this question happens to be no, then you could move to the next question, asking the candidate about the steps he or she would take if he or she had to handle a problem.

The Mediocre Question

(A) This is an okay question because it is a *situational* question. These are the questions where you ask, "What would you do 'if'...?"

The answer to this question reveals more about the way the candidate thinks through a process rather than what he or she has had experience with in the past. Listen to the answer to determine if he or she uses a systematic or a random way of thinking through problems.

The Weakest Question

(B) The answer you'll get to this question will be too broad and not specific enough to make a hiring decision. Any time there is a problem that is to be solved, the person must first think through the problem. Listen for the thinking process and determine whether this candidate is just answering the question or if the answer deals with the problem-solving process.

RATE YOURSELF

If you chose question **(C),** give yourself 5 points.

If you chose question **(A),** give yourself 3 points.

If you chose question **(B),** give yourself 0 points. _____

INTERVIEWER'S QUESTION

20. Learning how candidates work with others.

Select the strongest question—the one that will provide you with the most information.

(A) How would your coworkers describe you as a teammate?

(B) You haven't had any problem with coworkers in the past, have you?

(C) What are the three qualities you appreciate in a coworker?

I think the strongest question is _____.

ANSWERS

The Strongest Question

(A) This is the strongest question because candidates will speak through the words of others. This is called *third-party endorsement.*

For some candidates this question will be very challenging to answer because they haven't thought about how others see them. For other candidates it will be easier to "brag" or talk openly about themselves by saying what they think their coworkers would say about them. Either way, you will get information about the candidates and how they relate to others which can be clues as to how these candidates think on their feet.

The Mediocre Question

(C) With this question, you will learn some traits that the candidate considers important, particularly when he or she is relating to others. But you may get a laundry list, such as "They would say that I am hard-working, responsible, and very thorough." If this happens, you will have to ask for specifics. You will want to probe further and ask questions, such as, "Is there a specific reason they would say you were hard-working?"

The Weakest Question

(B) This is the weakest question because it is prompting the candidates to answer the way you want them to. You are almost saying, "Give me a no answer, and we can move forward."

It would be unlikely that candidates would disagree with you and say, "As a matter of fact, I have problems with my coworkers on a continual basis." And, if they did, you would probably pull back and realize that this was definitely a *red flag.* This answer would be admitting to having problems in the past. If you use that as an indicator of future behavior, you will need to listen carefully for patterns of this type of conduct.

RATE YOURSELF

If you chose question **(A),** give yourself 5 points.

If you chose question **(C),** give yourself 3 points.

If you chose question **(B),** give yourself 0 points. _____

INTERVIEWER'S QUESTION

21. Learning a candidate's preferred work situation.
Select the strongest question—the one that will provide you with the most information.

(A) Describe your ideal work environment.

(B) What four things are important to you in the work environment?

(C) From what you've read about this job, what would you find most challenging?

I think the strongest question is _____.

ANSWERS

The Strongest Question

(C) This is the best way to ask this question because it will determine whether the candidate has done any research to find out about your company or the job. See how candidates respond without your providing information. If they are simply applying because there is an opening, this will be revealed in their answer. Are the aspects a candidate finds challenging and interesting key factors of the job?

The Mediocre Question

(B) This question is sufficient because it asks for a number of values that the candidate finds important. Listen to the answer and look for a match with your environment, your needs, and the candidate's expectations and goals. If the candidate is seeking a friendly environment and yours is not a friendly atmosphere, the chances are that the candidate will not be happy and therefore not stick around.

The Weakest Question

(A) This question asks candidates to "spin me a fairy tale." The candidates could say anything you want to hear. They could answer, "My goal is to work at a midsized company where clothing products are manufactured." And that just happens to describe your company. This may be their goal, but it could also be a rehearsed answer that is given to each company and is tweaked each time the question is asked. More probing is needed here.

This question would be more effective if you asked when candidates had been most satisfied with their work environment. That way you get a sense of whether your environment is a good fit.

RATE YOURSELF

If you chose question **(C)**, give yourself 5 points.

If you chose question **(B)**, give yourself 3 points.

If you chose question **(A)**, give yourself 0 points. _____

INTERVIEWER'S QUESTION

22. Uncovering a candidate's goals.

Select the strongest question—the one that will provide you with the most information.

(A) What do you see yourself doing in five years?

(B) What are your short-term and long-term goals?

(C) How does this job fit with your long-range plans?

I think the strongest question is _____.

ANSWERS

The Strongest Question

(B) This is the strongest question because it breaks the goals into a time frame that is realistic. A candidate can come prepared to say something like, "I plan to grow and develop and take on added responsibility and perhaps get into management." But that is not what you want to know right now. What you want to know is if the candidate has a plan that involves not only the future but the job that you are recruiting for.

The Mediocre Question

(C) This is an okay question because of the way it is framed. "How does this fit into your long-range plans?" In other words, is this job a step toward your goal—whatever that is? The weakest part of this question is that it could be answered with a yes or no. You could strengthen the information you get by probing or following up with a question such as:

- How will this job help reach your goal?

- What is it about this job that attracted you to our company?

The Weakest Question

(A) This question is old and tired. Think of what has happened in our world in the past five years. Who could have predicted some of the technological advances that have been made? Who could have guessed that offshore work would change the work lives of millions of people? With companies acquiring other companies almost daily, this question just doesn't hit.

RATE YOURSELF

If you chose question **(B),** give yourself 5 points.

If you chose question **(C),** give yourself 3 points.

If you chose question **(A),** give yourself 0 points. _____

INTERVIEWER'S QUESTION

23. Determining how long someone will stay with your company.

Select the strongest question—the one that will provide you with the most information.

(A) What concerns you about this company's future?

(B) Where do you think this industry or this company is heading?

(C) What do you hope to gain by working at this company?

I think the strongest question is _____.

ANSWERS

The Strongest Question

(C) This question is a great follow-up question to, "What are your goals?" The purpose of this question is to find out what the candidates are planning for their future careers and whether they plan to stay beyond a specific time period. This would be a good time to watch for red flags regarding how long this candidate plans to stay at the job. An example of a red flag answer is a goal that is very specific such as, "I want to be a director in charge of a department within five years."

That's a good answer only if it is realistic. The candidate has provided you with information that you need to process. "Can we realistically expect this goal to be realized?" "Is it possible for this candidate to rise to that level in that amount of time?"

If the answer is no, you and the candidate should discuss the fact that your company has no plans to promote to that level in the next five years.

The Mediocre Question

(A) This question can help determine whether the candidate knows anything about the company's goals, but it doesn't tell you much about how long the candidate plans to stay with you. There is no excuse for someone coming to an interview without first doing research on the company. The Internet has many sources of information about companies, including annual earnings, founder's information, and the Web site. Some candidates may request an annual report before the interview. It will be your job to determine how much research about the company and position the candidate has done.

The Weakest Question

(B) This is the weakest question because it asks, "What do you think?" rather than, "What research have you done?" While the question is relevant, at this point you should be more interested in the candidate's skills than his or her opinions. A stronger approach would be to ask a direct question, such as, "What attracted you to this posting/company?"

RATE YOURSELF

If you chose question **(C),** give yourself 5 points.

If you chose question **(A),** give yourself 3 points.

If you chose question **(B),** give yourself 0 points. _____

INTERVIEWER'S QUESTION

24. Learning why the applicant wants to work for your company.

Select the strongest question—the one that will provide you with the most information.

(A) What is it that interests you most about this position/company?

(B) What attracted you to this particular job posting?

(C) How would you compare this position to your current or last position?

I think the strongest question is _____.

ANSWERS

The Strongest Question

(C) This is a strong yet basic question that reveals what the candidates liked about their last position and how that position compares to the position you are seeking to fill. This is a great opportunity to follow up with probing questions such as: "If there was one thing you could change from your last position, what would it be?"

The deeper you probe into this answer and follow up on the answers given, the more information you will have as to why the candidates are not content where they currently are or where they were. You will need to determine what makes them think that they will be content at your company and for how long.

The Mediocre Question

(A) You may find that the answer to this question will not reveal any specific information unless you probe to get it. Depending on the answer the candidate gives, you can determine what is interesting to the candidate and in turn can take this answer down many roads. Stronger questions to ask are:

- What responsibilities of the job would you find most interesting?

- What would you find most challenging about this position?

The Weakest Question

(B) This question won't reveal much relevant information about the candidate. A stronger way of asking the question would be, "What did you see as a match between your skills and the requirements of the job when you saw our job posting?"

RATE YOURSELF

If you chose question **(C)**, give yourself 5 points.

If you chose question **(A)**, give yourself 3 points.

If you chose question **(B)**, give yourself 0 points. _____

INTERVIEWER'S QUESTION

25. Determining why someone left, or is leaving, his or her last position.

Select the strongest question—the one that will provide you with the most information.

(A) On a scale of one to ten, how satisfied are you with your current job?

(B) Is there a particular reason that you are leaving your job at this time?

(C) How long ago did you decide to leave your position?

I think the strongest question is _____.

ANSWERS

The Strongest Question

(B) This question is the strongest because of the last three words: "at this time." Many candidates will answer the question, "Why are you leaving your job?" by stating that they are seeking a "new challenge." By adding the words "at this time," you are asking for a specific piece of information. You are basically asking, "Why now?" You are looking for an answer that will indicate if there was something specific happening at the company that would make the person want to leave now.

The Mediocre Question

(C) The difference between asking, "Is there a particular reason?" and, "How long ago did you decide?" is to find out whether this person has been unhappy in his or her job for a while, or whether something occurred recently that made him or her decide to leave.

If candidates have been thinking of leaving for three or four months or more, they may have burned out on the job or they may be dissatisfied with the work or their boss or coworkers. Those are good reasons to leave a job as long as candidates don't bring those problems to your company.

If, on the other hand, someone had a "blow up" or a specific reason for leaving at this particular time, then you will want to find out what happened. You will need more facts to find out if there is a problem. Was it a mutually agreeable parting?

The Weakest Question

(A) This question is not a good one to ask because it can be answered with a single number. It will require follow-up probing to determine what the rating is about and the reason candidates didn't rate themselves higher or the reason that they rated themselves as high as they did. It is much more effective to ask a direct question about the candidate's performance than to try to determine what a score of 8 means. A better question to ask would be: "What types of feedback did you get from your last boss or on your latest performance review?"

RATE YOURSELF

If you chose question **(B),** give yourself 5 points.

If you chose question **(C),** give yourself 3 points.

If you chose question **(A),** give yourself 0 points. _____

Test Two: Behavioral-Based Questions (26–50)

Behavioral-based questions ask for specific examples from a candidate that reveal his or her past behavior on the job. Using past behavior is a proven technique for accurately determining the future performance or success of an individual. In other words, if the candidate did it before, he or she may do it again. This applies to both positive and negative behavior. If candidates were top performers in their last job, the chances are good that they will be top performers in your company.

The difference between a behavioral question and a general question is that the behavioral question asks for a specific example. Behavioral questions usually begin with a request such as, "Tell me about a time when . . . ," or "Describe a situation in which . . . ."

To reap the benefits of the behavioral style of questioning, you will have to ask questions that require a very specific example of past behavior. You are basically asking the candidate to tell you a success story.

An example of a behavioral question is, "Tell me about a time when you solved a problem." The key words here are "a time." This answer calls for a *specific* example of a *specific* incident.

Any candidate can claim to be good at anything, but when you ask for an example of a detailed incident, you are asking for proof of past behavior—an example of a time when the candidate actually did what he or she is claiming. In other words, behavioral questions say, "Prove it by giving me an example."

There is a formula to be followed when asking behavioral questions. You want the candidates to tell you:

- What the problem or situation was.

- What action they took to resolve the situation or problem.

- What the outcome or result was.

One way to follow this model is by asking the behavioral question in three parts:

- Can you give me an example of a time when . . . ?

- I want to hear what the problem or situation was and what you did about it.

- What was the result?

If the candidate fails to give these parts in his or her example, you will need to probe further to get the whole story.

INTERVIEWER'S QUESTION

26. Tell me about a time when you solved a problem by thinking creatively.

Which of these responses actually answers the question? Which answer should you be wary of? Are there any red flags?

(A) "That would be my experience with branding. We hired some star athletes to brand our product. We sold the brand name, and everything we did pushed the name. We bought mailing lists and sent out thousands of ads through the mail. We spent a fair share of our budget pushing the brand. Every activity revolved around this brand we were trying to establish. Everyone in the company bought into the concept. It was a huge success, and we all celebrated our accomplishment."

(B) "When I started at my last company, there was a lack of customer retention. I worked with my staff and members of other relevant departments. The first thing I did was to form teams that went out and interviewed customers. I reviewed the data collected and compiled a spread sheet that I presented to the marketing department. I worked closely with the marketing team to develop a plan of action. We ended up with a successful strategy to 'ask customers first, sending information only upon request.' The key to the success of this program was getting buy-in from my team and giving my 100 percent support to the campaign from the very beginning."

(C) "I usually keep up with what's going on in the general market, and I sometimes have to act fast to get market share. We were trying to get attention in a fast-paced environment. I usually spend a great deal of work around budget, attempting to maximize leverage. I've been known to buy some premium advertising to get the word out. I've led some pretty successful campaigns, even when market conditions have not been in our favor."

I think the strongest answer is _____.

ANSWERS

The Strongest Answer

(B) This is the strongest answer because it is specific to a particular project. As the interviewer you can hear the action steps
taken and the role of leadership this person has demonstrated.
From this answer, you learn that the applicant appears to be a
person who has the ability to work with the smaller details
while maintaining the big-picture perspective. You will want
to ask for more examples to see if there is a pattern to indicate
that these factors are consistent.

The Mediocre Answer

(A) If you look back at the answer, you can count seven we's and no
I's. Although it is important to show a strong team function,
there should be some sign of the person's role. What do you
know about the person's role in this activity with this answer?

You will need to probe about the individual's role to find out
if he or she was a leader or follower and what part he or she
played in the success.

The Weakest Answer

(C) There are several red flags in this answer. First, the answer
does not address the question because there is no specific project sited. It is a lot of general information that doesn't tell you
anything about the candidate specifically.

Your probing should begin by getting a specific example
from the candidate. If this is not possible, and sometimes it is
not, then you will have to ask very specific questions about the
details, such as:

- What do you mean when you say, "I've led some pretty successful campaigns?"

- Can you give me an example of one of the campaigns?

Only after probing will you have an idea of what this individual has done in the past.

RATE YOURSELF

If you chose answer **(B)**, give yourself 5 points.

If you chose answer **(A)**, give yourself 3 points.

If you chose answer **(C)**, give yourself 0 points. _____

INTERVIEWER'S QUESTION

27. Describe a time when you had to adapt to a new situation.
Which response actually answers the question? Which answer should you be wary of? Are there any red flags?

(A) "I've become quite accustomed to new situations in the IT industry. I have been laid off twice in the last five years. In fact, one of the companies closed the doors as we walked out. I've had to accept the fact that not all start-up companies are going to make it."

(B) "My military background has prepared me for this part of any job. When you have been on call day and night and responsible for your unit's safety, you learn to be adaptable and flexible. Being flexible in the service is not only necessary, it is mandatory. I bring that same set of skills and sense of urgency to any job. I do whatever it takes to get the job done."

(C) "I was on call 24/7 one weekend. When the phone rang on Sunday morning, I knew there was a problem. Sure enough, there was a mainframe that went down. The first thing I did was to cancel my plans for the day. I responded to the call within one hour. I teamed up with three technicians to get the system up and running before Monday morning. We each had a responsibility but worked as a unit. We stayed until 2:00 a.m. When the employees arrived at work that morning, they weren't aware that there had been a problem. We got high kudos for responding so quickly."

I think the strongest answer is _____.

ANSWERS

The Strongest Answer

(C) This is the strongest answer because it answers the question with a specific example of adapting to a situation. As the interviewer you can hear how flexible this candidate is when she describes canceling plans and getting to the scene within an hour. This answer also shows how well this person works with others. This person's willingness to stay until 2:00 a.m. should convince you that this person is dedicated to getting the job done.

The Mediocre Answer

(B) While this is a good answer, it is mediocre because it does not give an example of a specific situation. You get a sense of the adaptability of this person and he has experience responding to new and unexpected situations, but you will need to hear a specific example to ensure that this is not just talk with no action. In other words, is this a tale instead of an example?

The Weakest Answer

(A) This answer doesn't show how this person adapted to something that was within her control. It is not a bad answer because there was adapting to a new job when she was laid off, but she did not adapt to a situation where her actions would have made a difference.

This answer is more about accepting and moving on than it is about adapting. Anyone can get laid off and adapt to not getting a paycheck, but what he or she did to take control of a situation is more important. You will need to probe for more information about how this person adapted to the new situation. A red flag to watch for is not so much that this person was laid off, but the decisions she has been making about the companies she chooses to work for. Did she do research before she accepted the job? Would she have accepted the job if she had known the facts she needed to know about the company? You will want to find out if this person thrives on change or if she has just had a run of bad luck. In other words, how long is she going to stick around?

RATE YOURSELF

If you chose answer (C), give yourself 5 points, _____

If you chose answer (B), give yourself 3 points, _____

If you chose answer (A), give yourself 0 points, _____

INTERVIEWER'S QUESTION

28. Can you give me an example of a time when you were working on a project that required sustained and persistent effort?

Which response actually answers the question? Which answer should you be wary of? Are there any red flags?

(A) "I have handled all assignments with the same amount of effort. I do whatever it takes to get the job done. If I haven't been able to get my job done during the day, I will stay late to complete whatever it is that didn't get accomplished. I pride myself on getting the job done whatever it takes."

(B) "The assignment that comes to mind is when I had a deadline to meet that would take three days to complete and I only had two days. What I did was to prioritize and delegate to other team members what I could. After that I worked steadily by blocking off hours to work on nothing but the project. At the same time I still had to get my regular work done. I put in a lot of extra hours, but for the most part, planning and prioritizing made a huge difference, and I got the job done on time."

(C) "I think the most sustained and persistent effort that I ever made was when I established a database for my last company. It was tedious work, and I had to work continuously or I would lose the momentum of getting the task done. I am pretty good at concentrating when I have to. I got through the project and did a good job, but I was glad to be over with that tedious task."

I think the strongest answer is _____.

ANSWERS

The Strongest Answer

(B) This is the strongest answer for several reasons. First the candidate listened to the question and answered what was asked: "Can you give me an example of a time when ...?" The question asks for "an example of a time when," and this answer gives a good example. The candidate also demonstrated the key qualities of planning, teamwork, and prioritizing. And the candidate displayed an attitude of being willing to do whatever it takes to get the job done, as well as the ability to do it in a smart manner.

The Mediocre Answer

(A) Although the answer fails to go into specifics, this is an okay answer because the candidate shares good information and has the right energy behind it. The phrase, "I always do whatever it takes to get the job done," would require some probing to get to a specific example of the behavior. If the candidate cannot give a specific example, perhaps the words are empty and claim something that may not be quite true.

The Weakest Answer

(C) This answer is weak for a couple of reasons. First, it shows that the candidate lacks confidence through the use of words such as "pretty good." Candidates are either good or not good. It also has the tone of someone who had to make a real effort to get through a tedious task. Depending on the job that this person is interviewing for, you will have to determine whether he or she will burn out from the types of tasks that will be performed in this position. The answer will require further probing to find out if this is a pattern of behavior or just boredom with this particular task. Consider asking, "What happened to the other work that had to be completed while you were so focused on this task?"

RATE YOURSELF

If you chose answer **(B)**, give yourself 5 points.

If you chose answer **(A)**, give yourself 3 points.

If you chose answer **(C)**, give yourself 0 points. _____

INTERVIEWER'S QUESTION

29. **Would you give me an example of a time when you worked on a project that required a great deal of written communication?**

    Which response actually answers the question? Which answer should you be wary of? Are there any red flags?

    (A) "That would be when I took over the responsibility of writing the department newsletter. This was my first experience at co-ordinating a publication from start to finish by myself. The first thing I did was to consult with the people in the company who had written similar newsletters to get a sense of what to do and what not to do. Next, I did an informal survey of company employees, everyone from the support staff to the director of the department. From their comments I came up with a new idea of getting the people involved. Now, each month I hold a writing contest and then publish the winner's stories. The employee involvement has made a big difference in my efforts. Recently, the newsletter was awarded "most creative departmental newsletter.""

    (B) "My writing skills have always been my strong point. I have been commended on my writing ability in every performance review that I have ever had. I am very good at researching facts and following through on leads. In my last job I was involved in the creation of our Web site by writing the content. That was a great experience. Working closely with the designers, I was able to contribute and add to the message that they were trying to get across."

    (C) "Writing isn't the major focus of my job responsibilities, but I do like to write very much. I have written some proposals, and they have been received very well. When I do have writing assignments, it is usually in addition to my regular job. I can tell you that whenever I have had the opportunity to write, I have received several comments on what a good job I have done. In fact, I was given an award for my writing skills as a team member on a project that received a grant. I am looking at this job as a chance to learn and develop my writing skills."

I think the strongest answer is ____.

ANSWERS

The Strongest Answer

(A) This answer provides a solid example of using written communication on a project. It's also a good answer because if you listen carefully, you can spot other qualities and skills beyond written communication. She did research about past successes and failures, as well as conducting an informal survey; both tasks involve verbal communication skills. She also thought outside the box and came up with a new idea to involve others, which demonstrates collaboration and team spirit.

The Mediocre Answer

(B) This answer is mediocre because although it alludes to a project, it really doesn't share any specific details about the project. The answer starts out with very general comments about performance appraisals but no real information as to what the candidate was writing or what the commendation was.

  The answer also alludes to a project involving content for the company's Web site, but it doesn't provide information on how much content was written or how original the writing was. At face value this is an answer without much bite. Depending on what percentage of the job will require written communication skills, you should probe further to find out the details. To get the facts, say, "I'd like to hear more information about the remarks on your performance appraisal. Could you give me an example of the comments or projects that you were working on?"

The Weakest Answer

(C) This answer is weak not because the person doesn't have the experience, but because of the lack of specific examples. You will have to probe to find more out about the award for the writing skills when working with a team. How much of a contribution did this person make to the team effort?

  The red flag in this answer is the fact that this person wants to "learn and develop." Hiring someone in order to teach and motivate him or her is probably not what you had in mind when you went looking for a person with writing skills.

RATE YOURSELF

If you chose answer **(A),** give yourself 5 points.

If you chose answer **(B),** give yourself 3 points.

If you chose answer **(C),** give yourself 0 points. _____

INTERVIEWER'S QUESTION

30. **Tell me about a time when you used strategic thinking to solve a problem.**

    Which response actually answers the question? Which answer should you be wary of? Are there any red flags?

    (A) "At my last company I developed a strategic plan that reduced the payroll costs by 8 percent in the first year. It involved developing and implementing ongoing efficiency training."

    (B) "I was the project manager responsible for the implementation of a project with a tight deadline. Unfortunately, in the middle of everything we had a problem with one of our computer systems. The first thing I did was to research and find the problem. I consulted with the IT department and shared my research with them. Based on the recommendations of the experts, I put together a plan to attack the problem. We were able to retrace the breakdown and determine the source and solution with a minimum amount of downtime. We met the deadline but had to put in some extra hours to accomplish the task."

    (C) "I have led the strategic planning team for my company that successfully generated $3 million over the last quarter. My responsibility was to build a long-range strategic plan. I worked with a diverse team and came up with plans that have been extremely successful. We implemented a state-of-the-art information system to automate core business. This was met with great enthusiasm and support and was a huge success."

I think the strongest answer is _____.

ANSWERS

The Strongest Answer

(B) This answer demonstrates a number of skills while answering the question asked. Some of the skills that can be extracted from this example are leadership, research, problem solving, communication, interpersonal skills, team work and collaboration, organizational skills, and a dedication to meeting deadlines.

Sometimes it's not the answer that is strong or weak, it is the skills that you can identify from the story told. This is a good example of answering the question asked in a format that tells the whole story. For example:

- *The problem/situation:* a computer system had a problem.

- *The action*: many steps and consultations performed in order to come to a solution.

- *The result:* determination of the source of the problem and a fix for it.

The Mediocre Answer

(C) Any interviewer would be interested in the statement, "successfully generated $3 million over the last quarter." But the details of generating that money are somewhat vague. As a manager, you are left wondering what was it about the project that was so state-of-the-art? What kind of a team is a "diverse team"?

The Weakest Answer

(A) This is the weakest as well as the shortest answer. More facts are needed. Although your attention may have been drawn to the reduction in costs, you don't really know much about the plan used and whether that sort of money reduction is feasible at your company. More probing will reveal the type of methods used to reduce costs and some of the points of the strategic plan that made it a success.

RATE YOURSELF

If you chose answer **(B),** give yourself 5 points.

If you chose answer **(C),** give yourself 3 points.

If you chose answer **(A),** give yourself 0 points. _____

INTERVIEWER'S QUESTION

31. Tell me about a time when you dealt with an angry customer.

Which response actually answers the question? Which answer should you be wary of? Are there any red flags?

(A) "I am a strong believer in good customer service. I believe that the customer is always right, and I will work to achieve results whenever possible. Every once in a while I will get an angry customer, and I am insulted by the way that I am treated. I understand that they are angry, but I do not understand why they take it out on us customer service reps. It's when they want to keep telling me how badly they've been treated that I cannot deal with them. If I can see that the person is beyond being reasonable, I will escalate the call to someone at a higher level to deal with that customer."

(B) "One day I received a call from a very angry man who had been passed from one service technician to another. By the time he was passed to me, he was beyond civil. He was yelling and threatening me. The first thing that I did was to stay calm, and in a confident voice I assured him that I would work with him to get the problem solved. He continued to vent while I listened to the details of his situation. I assured him that I was there to help him through to the end. I supplied my contact info and told him I would call him back within the hour. I quickly researched the facts and found the problem. I called him back and asked him some questions to clarify the facts. I was able to walk him through his problem. To say he was thankful would be an understatement."

(C) "I received the customer service award for excellence in my company for two years straight. I try to treat customers the way I would want to be treated. I try to listen to their problems and then to find out the facts. I ask a lot of questions to make sure that I have all the details and then do research to put the pieces together. Because I am a person who is very organized, I can pull together the facts and usually come up with a solution. I have had to take complaints and even verbal abuse a couple of times, but I figure that's just pure frustration talking. It gives me a good feeling when I do solve a customer's problem and they are grateful to me for the good service."

I think the strongest answer is _____.

ANSWERS

The Strongest Answer

(B) This answers the request for a specific example as well as demonstrates the candidate's ability to deal with difficult customers while staying calm and dealing with whatever is given. There is a sense of confidence and a positive demeanor in the description of how this candidate took control of the situation when others had not. This answer takes you through the step-by-step process that resulted in success with a satisfied customer. If this is how he solved problems in the past, it is a good indicator of how he will treat your customers in the future. You could delve deeper to find out if there is a pattern of control and confidence in dealing with customers, especially difficult ones, in all his answers.

The Mediocre Answer

(C) This answer contains the right information, but it does not answer the question and it is not specific. It is vague about a lot of the details, and it requires follow-up questions to see if there is fact behind the claims.

   The strongest statement in this answer is the fact that she received the customer service award for excellence in her company for two years. One probing question would be to find out when those awards were given. A recent award will weigh more heavily than if it was received five or more years ago.

The Weakest Answer

(A) This is the weakest answer because you know very little about this person or his work habits at the end of this answer. There is nothing specific here—just a lot of talk about "beliefs," but nothing to substantiate the beliefs.

   A red flag in this answer is when the candidate felt "insulted" when he was attacked by an angry customer. Depending on the type of problems this person will be handling, it should be noted that he can, or does, take things personally. This answer could signal that this person survives well in a "perfect world," but you should find out what happens when the world is reality-based.

RATE YOURSELF

If you chose answer **(B),** give yourself 5 points.

If you chose answer **(C),** give yourself 3 points.

If you chose answer **(A),** give yourself 0 points. _____

INTERVIEWER'S QUESTION

32. Describe a time when you had to make an unpopular decision.

Which response actually answers the question? Which answer should you be wary of? Are there any red flags?

(A) "In my job as a project manager I worked with a team of technicians, and it was my task to find cost-cutting measures. This included laying off personnel. I labored over my decision to make sure that I was being objective. I analyzed each person and his or her role in the project. In the end I was asked to cut staff by 20 percent. I prepared my list based on my careful planning. I was the one who had to tell each person the job was being cut. I felt I had treated the situation as fairly as I could, but I must admit it was a very tough task to announce the layoffs to my staff."

(B) "There was a time when I decided to hire an external candidate for a job that several internal candidates had applied for. Many people were upset with my decision and let me know about it. In fact, one person actually was upset enough to go to human resources and claim that she was discriminated against. I defended my decision to people who complained and tried to justify my decision. I had to do what I felt was in the best interest of the department. I felt like I had picked an excellent candidate and stood by my decision."

(C) "Sometimes a manager has to make unpopular decisions. That's what we get paid to do—to think outside the box and make decisions. I've made some difficult decisions over my career, and some were the right decisions and some the wrong decisions. If I think something is wrong, I will let you know about it. I'm not a person who lets things pile up. I try to act on the problem as soon after it happened as possible."

I think the strongest answer is _____.

ANSWERS

The Strongest Answer

(A) This is a great example of a time when a tough decision had to be made. As the interviewer you can hear that although telling people that their jobs were over was not pleasant, it was dealt with objectively. The tone of the answer indicates that this was done in a very careful and caring manner. It also shows careful preparation with the planning of the task. This answer also demonstrates strength in the ability to do whatever it takes to get the job done.

The Mediocre Answer

(B) This answer does not give any specifics about the candidate herself. She made the decision, but you as the interviewer do not know why she made the decision or what criteria she used to justify not hiring the internal candidates. You know that one person went to HR to complain, and you know that people were upset with her, but you don't know much more than that. You will need to find out more information by probing. Try asking, "What made you hire the external candidate?" or "What criteria did you use to rule out the internal candidates?"

The Weakest Answer

(C) This is the weakest answer because it does not answer the question. It starts out with a statement and then carries that statement through the answer. A red flag is the statement, "some were the wrong decisions." If you hear an answer like this, probe further to find out if the wrong decisions were well thought out or made in the spur of the moment.

RATE YOURSELF

If you chose answer **(A)**, give yourself 5 points.

If you chose answer **(B)**, give yourself 3 points.

If you chose answer **(C)**, give yourself 0 points. _____

INTERVIEWER'S QUESTION

33. Tell me about a time when you took the initiative concerning something that you saw needed to be done.

Which response gives a specific answer to the question? Which answer should you be wary of? Are there any red flags?

(A) "As an officer in the military I had many occasions to initiate action. There was one time when I had to make a quick decision that made the difference as to whether or not lives were saved. A signal that should have been given was not, and as a result there were men being shot at who shouldn't have been in that situation. By making an independent decision, I called a cease-fire. I was able to stop the action and keep my troops from being seriously injured or killed that day."

(B) "I am a person who tries to plan ahead, and so I usually have a planned schedule for every step of a project. There was a time when my plan started to come undone because of unforeseen events. What I did was to stop all activities until I could regroup. If I had let things progress, I could see that we were not going to have the end results we needed to finish the project. As it turned out, we did complete the project, and my plan was completed as I had hoped it would be."

(C) "As a project manager for my last company, I could see a need for a template to guide team members through projects. I worked on a prototype and presented it to my manager. He liked the idea and encouraged me to follow up on the idea and develop it. I made some changes based on my team's suggestions. When I had it produced, the team was delighted to have a format to assist them in organizing their tasks. My boss presented it to management, and it is now used companywide. I received an award for initiating a more efficient process that will save time and ultimately money."

I think the strongest answer is _____.

ANSWERS

The Strongest Answer

(C) This is the best answer for many reasons. It gives a specific example of a time when the candidate actually took initiative and follows the structure to allow you as the interviewer to see the action taken to complete the task. The ending of this example is especially impressive because the candidate not only was rewarded for his initiative, but he determined that the process will save time and money. Wouldn't you want to hear more from this person to find out what other time- and money-saving ideas he had initiated?

The Mediocre Answer

(A) This is a mediocre answer not because of the content, but because it leaves you with unanswered questions. There is no doubt that there was a quick decision made and an initiative taken, but what happened in between is somewhat of a mystery. Quick thinking and judgment are skills that any job would require. However, you will have to probe deeper to peel away the layers to understand this example and uncover more necessary details about what happened.

The Weakest Answer

(B) This answer really misses the mark as far as initiating an action is concerned. In fact, this answer is so vague that it is difficult to see what the person was trying to accomplish other than follow her plan. In fact, the answer gives very little information other than sharing that the candidate is a planner and likes to have things follow a plan. This could be a red flag, showing that this person may lack flexibility and not be able to shift gears when things go wrong. You will need to probe to find out what the action of "stopping all activities" would cost in the way of time and staff and whether there were other, less drastic steps that could have been taken.

RATE YOURSELF

If you chose answer **(C),** give yourself 5 points.

If you chose answer **(A),** give yourself 3 points.

If you chose answer **(B),** give yourself 0 points. _____

INTERVIEWER'S QUESTION

34. Give me an example of an obstacle you faced and how you overcame it.

Which response actually answers the question? Which answer should you be wary of? Are there any red flags?

(A) "There was a woman at my last job who was known to be difficult to work with. I decided early on that I was not going to cross this woman. I figured she had a problem, and I didn't want to make that problem mine. I figured if I treated her with the same respect and courtesy as I treat any coworker or customer she wouldn't have reason to give me a bad time. As a result, we were able to work with one another without any problems."

(B) "I volunteer for a group of kids with disabilities and coach them to play basketball. Last year my team didn't seem to understand the meaning of the word 'team.' I decided rather than preach to them that I would take them out for some fun together. We all went out for pizza one evening and sat around and got to know each other by sharing stories and experiences. They seemed to let down their guard when we were off of the court. It was a real bonding experience, and surprisingly it carried over when they were playing the game. We ate a lot of pizza that year and finished in a decent spot in the league. But most of all it was a growth experience for each team member, and that's what I thought mattered."

(C) "When I was a college student, I was assigned to a group to work on a project together. There were five other members, and we were working on a science project that was about the effects of mold and bacteria. We had to complete the project by the end of the term. One of the challenges was that we all had different schedules and had a really difficult time getting together. Only one other student and I were science majors, so the rest of the students were looking to us to lead the project. So I talked to the other science student, and we decided that we would delegate tasks to the other team members to get the project done. That way no one else would have to do research, and everyone could handle the workload. We had a great project in the end and got a good grade for our efforts."

I think the strongest answer is _____.

ANSWERS

The Strongest Answer

(B) This is the strongest answer because it provides a specific example. It's a good story full of action that you can see and hear. This candidate demonstrated not only overcoming obstacles but also taking a creative approach to a problem and motivating a team in the process.

The fact that the person does volunteer work with special children should be an indicator that this person is willing to go above and beyond what is expected. There is also evidence that this person has patience and is willing to try new solutions to get an issue resolved.

The Mediocre Answer

(A) This is an okay answer because it gives an example of an obstacle: a difficult-to-get-along-with coworker. It reveals the result of the candidate's handling of the problem, but it doesn't provide specific details about how the candidate actually overcame the obstacle. By probing, you could get more details and find out if it went as smoothly as stated in this example. Follow-up questions could be:

- Was there a time when you had to bite your tongue to get along with this person, or did she just change her behavior because of the way you treated her?

- What was the reaction of your coworkers when they saw that you had "special" treatment by this woman?

The Weakest Answer

(C) This is the weakest answer because it tells more about the project and the problems than about how the candidate prioritized to get through his busy schedule. When a candidate rambles on about insignificant details, you will have to either stop him and refocus the example or do a good job of probing to follow up on the actual action taken to solve this problem.

RATE YOURSELF

If you chose answer **(B),** give yourself 5 points.

If you chose answer **(A),** give yourself 3 points.

If you chose answer **(C),** give yourself 0 points. _____

INTERVIEWER'S QUESTION

35. Can you give me an example of a time when your leadership made a difference in your current or previous job?
Which response actually answers the question? Which answer should you be wary of? Are there any red flags?

(A) "Leadership has been a role that I have assumed in every job I've ever held. My last position was as general manager of the entire East Coast. My strength lies in my communication skills. I learned early in my career that you have to communicate to reach out to the various customers you serve; that includes internal as well as external customers. I am a believer in giving praise and rewards for a job well done."

(B) "As national sales operations manager I trained, developed, and lead a 20-person national sales account and support team targeting the textile industry worldwide. I led the team in strategic and tactical leadership. We were extremely successful in the installations of state-of-the-art technology. We had a record sales year every year that I was there; the team pulling together made the difference. I think any member of my team would tell you that I am a leader they would work for anytime. We really had a very successful team spirit."

(C) "When I took over my role as CEO for a retail chain, I was in full charge of strategic planning and operations. The first thing I did was to hold a meeting with my staff to find out best practices of the company. I let staff members do most of the talking. I find that good communication includes good listening skills. After the meeting I had a transcription of everything that was said and summarized it on a spreadsheet. In our second meeting I revealed my plans and how the suggestions they had made would be incorporated. I can honestly say that I have never had a more solid relationship with my staff members. Including them in the planning made a huge difference in the success of the project."

I think the strongest answer is _____.

ANSWERS

The Strongest Answer

(C) This example shows strong communication skills being demonstrated through listening as well as talking. The answer also shows that this person can work collaboratively rather than just take over a project. It would appear from this answer that this candidate's ego does not depend on his getting the recognition or credit for the project.

   This is the person who will come into your company and will work with your existing staff members. Is this the type of attitude you think your team would work well with? If so, probe for more examples of successes that came about by working collaboratively. You will want to find out about the challenges that he overcame to get the team working together with a new leader.

The Mediocre Answer

(B) This answer has all the right components of success but none of the specifics. The answer clearly talks of leadership and responsibility but doesn't have any facts to back the statements made.

   This is where some skilled probing will make a difference in finding out whether this person has been as successful as she claims. To learn more about this person's leadership abilities, consider probing with questions such as, "Could you give me an example of the training and development you did for your team members?"

The Weakest Answer

(A) This is the weakest answer because it lacks focus and does not answer the question. When a candidate generalizes, you will have to ask probing questions to get a specific example. Try asking, "Could you give me an example of how you communicated with your staff on a particular project?"

RATE YOURSELF

If you chose answer **(C),** give yourself 5 points.

If you chose answer **(B),** give yourself 3 points.

If you chose answer **(A),** give yourself 0 points. _____

INTERVIEWER'S QUESTION

36. Describe your experience working with global markets by giving me an example of a project you worked on.

Which response actually answers the question? Which answer should you be wary of? Are there any red flags?

(A) "I provided technical problem resolution and ensured effective coordination of activities in every job that I have held regardless of what market I have worked in. I have also gained a reputation within the manufacturing industry as a key player when it comes to hard bargaining and negotiating both nationally and internationally. In my last two jobs I was able to save the companies several thousands of dollars by negotiating savvy business deals."

(B) "I was involved in a project in which I had to work closely with an international team to collaborate the planning of technical standards. Because there was a nine-hour time difference, we agreed on times that would be agreeable to both teams for regular meetings. Next, we agreed to use whatever technology was available to us. If we weren't e-mailing or faxing, we had a lot of telephone conferences and some video meetings. Whenever we had a meeting, I would make sure that several types of communication were used in case one hadn't conveyed the message. We managed to handle the entire project on a virtual basis with no travel. This was a big cost savings decision, and it allowed us the flexibility to do more than one project. In the end we all agreed that the project was a real growth experience."

(C) "My knowledge and experience in this industry encompasses a total of 10 years. I see real value in my years of experience with a company that has similar customers and contacts. I have a broad scope of experience and expertise to pull from to analyze and solve problems of a broad scope. I have worked with Fortune 500 companies as well as small start-ups, both in local and larger global markets. I have also built strong relationships throughout my career that will help me hit the ground running at this company."

I think the strongest answer is _____.

ANSWERS

The Strongest Answer

(B) This answer provides excellent specific examples of leadership and collaboration as well as accommodation. The answer gives the impression that the person is not only savvy in working with global diversity but with the technology as well to overcome the differences of time and space. In addition, by holding "virtual" meetings, there was significant money saved. This person clearly thinks through every aspect of a project.

The Mediocre Answer

(C) This answer not only fails to address the question but is too broad with no real examples to back up the claims made. There is also no mention of working in the global market.

However, on the surface, at least, the answer has good content. The candidate sums up what he has to offer with his years of experience, the breadth of companies he worked for, as well as his wealth of resources and knowledge of the industry.

The Weakest Answer

(A) This is the weakest answer because it rambles on without any purpose. It is very vague and definitely not a specific answer to the question.

"I provided technical problem resolution and ensured effective coordination of activities in every job that I have held regardless of what market I have worked in." This is a nice statement, but it doesn't say anything that would help you assess the behavior of this person. You will have to ask several probe questions to uncover what this person has done and what she has to offer. Consider asking, "Give an example of how you go about 'hard bargaining and negotiating.'"

RATE YOURSELF

If you chose answer **(B)**, give yourself 5 points.

If you chose answer **(C)**, give yourself 3 points.

If you chose answer **(A)**, give yourself 0 points. _____

INTERVIEWER'S QUESTION

37. Tell me about a time when you had a conflict with a boss or coworker.

Which response actually answers the question? Which answer should you be wary of? Are there any red flags?

(A) "When I was new at my last job, there was a coworker who was being rude to me and criticizing the way I was doing things. I am a usually very quick about picking up on new things, but in this situation I hadn't been trained. I decided to talk to her about the situation before it went any further. I asked her if we could have a meeting, and she reluctantly agreed. I told her that I respected the fact that she had been doing the job for some years and that I looked to her for guidance. She told me that it was not her role to teach the new people. I told her that I appreciated that but that if she would just point out the things that I was doing incorrectly and what I needed to do differently, I was sure that I would be able to be more helpful. I think she liked my attitude because things improved after that meeting."

(B) "There was a time when my boss was not taking action to discipline a coworker who was coming in late on a regular basis. I talked to him, and he basically told me that he was in charge and that I was to take responsibility for my own behavior and not my coworkers. I was really upset with his attitude. It seems to me that if there is a policy, then everyone should be expected to live by the same rules. I felt so strongly about it that I reported the incident to HR. My boss was upset that the HR manager became involved. I ended up leaving that job because of the lack of consistency in the treatment of employees."

(C) "I'm the type of person who doesn't ever have conflict at work. In fact I get along with everyone. I try to ignore people's irritating behavior and just mind my own business. I don't get into the gossip or talk that goes on in the office. If something upsets me, I just take a break or go for a walk and let myself cool down. I've worked with a lot of different people, and there have been plenty of times when I could have had conflicts with them, but I just don't think it is worth it. It would just upset me, and I am better off just focusing on my own work."

I think the strongest answer is _____.

ANSWERS

The Strongest Answer

(A) This is a very good example of dealing with conflict through communications. It answers the question and gives you good information about the person. There is a sense of politeness and respect about the conversation that this person had with her coworker. There is also a reference to being able to learn quickly that would be worth probing further to determine whether this person would be able to pick up the details of your job quickly. Sometimes when a candidate does not have experience but can learn quickly, it may be worth the investment of time and training to bring that person up to speed.

The Mediocre Answer

(B) The tone in this answer should be viewed as a red flag. It might reflect this candidate's inability to deal with gray areas. In other words, does she only see black and white? In this case she only saw that the policy was being broken, and she felt strongly enough to go the HR with the grievance even after she talked with her boss.

The possible red flag is this candidate's flexibility. Will her strict interpretation of policy be a problem? Or is this an indication of an employee who is strong enough to stand up for what she believes in? You will have to determine if this person is a good fit for your particular company's culture and the general standards for adhering to policy.

The Weakest Answer

(C) This answer is poor on many counts. First, the comments are very general, such as "I get along with everyone," and, "I'm the type of person who doesn't have conflict at work." While these are admirable statements, the candidate later contradicts herself by saying that there are plenty of times when there could have been conflicts. A red flag in this answer is that the candidate may react to problems with passive behavior instead of with assertive behavior by talking the problem out.

RATE YOURSELF

If you chose answer **(A),** give yourself 5 points.

If you chose answer **(B),** give yourself 3 points.

If you chose answer **(C),** give yourself 0 points. _____

INTERVIEWER'S QUESTION

38. Tell me about the biggest project you worked on from start to finish.

Which response actually answers the question? Which answer should you be wary of? Are there any red flags?

(A) "The company where I currently work received one of the biggest orders in its history. We were really excited about the order, and we all worked very hard to pull the whole project off. We had to design a new piece of equipment that required new materials and new resources. After many meetings we were able to streamline the process and combine some features of the product while still satisfying the customer. We worked long hours to pull the project together. In the end we not only satisfied the customer but exceeded expectations."

(B) "I was in charge of designing the Web site for our company. The first thing I did was to meet with the graphic design team and talk about ideas and possibilities. I next went to the marketing department and talked about the message we wanted to send. Both groups had lots of good ideas. I then did some research on what marketing principles worked best on the Internet. I came up with several ideas and then went back to my original contacts in graphics and marketing. They were enthusiastic about the direction I was taking and approved wholeheartedly. In the end it was a very successful project with a great deal of collaborative effort and guidance by the experts. I received many kudos for my coordination of the project."

(C) "I led the rollout of a new food product. It was to be featured in all major supermarkets. One of the important details of rolling out this product was the timing. If it was released too close to the holidays, it would get lost in all of the confusion in stores at that time of the year. If we waited until after the holidays, the slow season would begin, and we would have lost the opportunity to reach the target audience. We did studies and surveys and finally decided that the best timing was to it roll out in the fall when the weather starts to change and there is more time spent in the kitchen and home. We planned our campaign around the fall season. In fact, it surpassed expectations and sales for a rollout. I received a nice bonus for my work on the project."

I think the strongest answer is _____.

ANSWERS

The Strongest Answer
(B) This answer provides a solid example of a project that was successful and collaborative. The candidate follows the pattern of telling what the situation was and what his role in the project was. He then takes you, the interviewer, through the steps to move the project from inception to completion.

This answer reveals other skill sets this candidate possesses, such as communications skills, an ability to use research and resources from experts, coordinating the information, and bringing the project together.

The Mediocre Answer
(A) There is a problem with the story in this answer. It's a success story of a team pulling together to solve a problem; the only thing wrong with the story is that the candidate is missing.

The candidate uses the pronoun "we" six times but does not explain her role in the project. You will have to probe to find out the candidate's particular role in the project and how much she contributed to its success. Follow up with: "When you say 'we,' whom exactly are you referring to?"

The Weakest Answer
(C) This is the weakest answer because you know more about the product rollout at the end of the answer than you do about the candidate. This is a common problem among candidates. They tend to focus on the project itself rather than what part they played in it. Even if the candidate worked with a team, you need to know what role he played. You will have to probe to find out just who was making the decisions and how this affected the candidate.

RATE YOURSELF

If you chose answer **(B)**, give yourself 5 points.

If you chose answer **(A)**, give yourself 3 points.

If you chose answer **(C)**, give yourself 0 points. _____

INTERVIEWER'S QUESTION

39. Tell me about a time when you had to convince someone to do something that he or she did not want to do.

Which response actually answers the question? Which answer should you be wary of? Are there any red flags?

(A) "I had an idea to market a product using a new approach. The first thing I did was to put my idea on a PowerPoint presentation. Then I took it to my boss and showed her. She was somewhat reluctant, but I think she liked my enthusiasm and told me to go ahead with the development of my idea. I took it to the marketing department, and together we planned a great strategy including a direct mail campaign. I was the one responsible for figuring out the budget as well as projecting return on investment. I think I surprised everyone with the projection that I made. As it turned out, I got the go-ahead, and when we marketed my idea, it turned out to be an even bigger success than anyone, including me, anticipated."

(B) "My boss would tell you that I am always selling him on something. I have at least one idea a week. I will admit that some of my ideas are better than others. My success rate is about 80 to 85 percent as far as moneymakers go. When you work for a really big company, it takes weeks to get approval. I sometimes get really frustrated with the procedure because I'm the kind of guy who just wants to 'do it.'"

(C) "My current boss has not always been open to new ideas. I was, however, able to sell her on one of my ideas when I showed her a marketing plan that I had worked on. She approved it and encouraged me to move forward with it. Behind the scenes I put together tons of data and then analyzed the data. I typically do a great deal of research before I even think about presenting an idea. The downside of working for a big company is that it can take weeks to get any kind of a reply. This is the reason that I have decided to leave. I want to work at a midsized company like yours where I can present ideas and not have to wait weeks before I get an answer."

I think the strongest answer is _____.

ANSWERS

The Strongest Answer

(A) This is a good solid example of a step-by-step process of influencing a decision and then being able to implement an idea. It is also an example of thinking outside the box with a new idea.

This answer shows the candidate's other qualities such as taking the initiative with a PowerPoint presentation, and then using the presentation to influence her boss. There is also a sense of passion or enthusiasm for what she believed was a good idea. It was her enthusiasm and energy that swayed her boss, and that is a positive quality that the candidate can bring to any job.

The Mediocre Answer

(C) This answer is only average because it starts out well and then changes direction completely. The candidate initially provides a specific example but then turns to general information instead of telling the details about the project that the boss had approved. You will have to get the candidate back on track to find out what he did after the project got the the go-ahead.

This is a person who has a lot of ideas but obviously hasn't been encouraged to do this as part of his job. This could be a red flag because the candidate may be focusing on something that is not in his job responsibilities. You will have to probe to see if this is a problem that has come up before or something that has been encouraged and rewarded.

The Weakest Answer

(B) Although this answer has some good content, there is no example given. This person claims to have an "idea a week," but fails to talk specifically about the time when an idea was accepted. She also claims that her success rate is "80 to 85 percent as far as money-makers go." Does that mean that her ideas bring in money? You will have to ask more questions about the claim regarding her success rate.

RATE YOURSELF

If you chose answer **(A)**, give yourself 5 points.

If you chose answer **(C)**, give yourself 3 points.

If you chose answer **(B)**, give yourself 0 points. _____

INTERVIEWER'S QUESTION

40. **You say you have good customer service skills. Tell me about a time when your customer service skills helped you in a difficult situation.**

Which response actually answers the question? Which answer should you be wary of? Are there any red flags?

(A) "I've always been a person who believed in good customer service whatever the company or industry, so when I had the chance to get a certification in customer relationship management, I took advantage of the opportunity. I have an ability to work with people and the training certification I went through in CRM only increased my knowledge and ability. Anyone who works with me would tell you that I can smooth out the most difficult situations and have the customers calling to thank me for working with them. I truly think that good customer service is the name of the game. That goes for internal as well as external customers."

(B) "I resolved a customer problem that involved one of our sales reps and another company. I worked as a liaison between our rep and the corporate office. The rep was very upset that we were not standing behind our warranty on a product he sold to the company. The first thing I did was pull the appropriate paperwork, and then I made a recommendation to our corporate office based on my findings. I laid out the facts, and we had a negotiation. In the end everything turned out well for the rep and the customer. The rep couldn't thank me enough. He told me that I had saved the account."

(C) "In my nine years working with a variety of customers I have had many compliments on my customer service skills. Sometimes I work directly with the customer, sometimes I work with the salespeople, and sometimes I work as a connection between the sales people and the customer. Because I am a person who is very thorough, I can track several cases at the same time. I make sure that each person feels as though someone is on top of the situation and working on his or her behalf."

I think the strongest answer is _____.

ANSWERS

The Strongest Answer

(B) This candidate answers the question by telling of a time when her customer service skills helped in a difficult situation. When she stated on her résumé or told you that she had good customer service skills, she made a claim. When you as the interviewer asked her to prove it by giving you an example of a time when she demonstrated those skills, she provided you with past behavior as an indicator of future success. This is a good example of answering the question asked.

The Mediocre Answer

(C) While this answer provides examples of skills this person has, it does not answer the question nor does it point to a specific example of putting those skills into action. By asking probing questions, you can help this person to articulate a specific time when she worked with the customers or salespeople. If you probe and ask for an example of a time when she received one of the many compliments and she cannot come up with a specific example, then her claim falls flat.

The Weakest Answer

(A) This person doesn't come close to answering the question. There are a lot of theory and opinions in this answer, but it is not backed with any facts. Having education or a certificate is a good thing, but it will be only as good as the skills acquired to apply the knowledge. This answer may identify a person who is knowledgeable but who hasn't really put the techniques learned to the test of a real-life situation. To find out if this person has the right experience, try asking, "Give me an example of a call from a customer thanking you for your service. What exactly did you do for that customer?"

RATE YOURSELF

If you chose answer **(B)**, give yourself 5 points.

If you chose answer **(C)**, give yourself 3 points.

If you chose answer **(A)**, give yourself 0 points. _____

INTERVIEWER'S QUESTION

41. Give me an example of your working in a fast-paced environment.

Which response actually answers the question? Which answer should you be wary of? Are there any red flags?

(A) "That would be when I worked in a law firm. We were short-staffed, and I took on the responsibility of coordinating several of the cases and the reports that went along with them. The first thing I did was to sit down with each of the attorneys and discuss priorities. I then put together a spreadsheet to manage my time and the deadlines. I had to work until midnight a couple of nights, but I worked closely with the attorneys to make sure that they had what they needed on time. I really thrived on the experience. It was very challenging. Everyone was surprised by how smoothly it went. I am happy to say that I received a nice bonus as a reward for taking the initiative and keeping things running smoothly."

(B) "I thrive in a fast-paced environment. I like a good challenge, and meeting tight deadlines is always a challenge. There have been times when I have been involved in as many as 10 projects at the same time and have still been able to respond to the pressure and deliver results. One thing I've noticed is that I always learn from every project I work on. I just keep getting more adept at juggling projects. I've never had an assignment on which I haven't been able to meet the deadline. I think very quickly and make fast decisions with good judgment. Those skills, plus my computer ability, really make me a top performer under pressure."

(C) "I work on a lot of projects that have tight deadlines, and this means working under pressure. I remember one especially stressful project that seemed to be working out really well and then everything started to go wrong. We had a tight deadline, and we all had to work extra hours. There was a great deal of tension in the office, and at one point I just felt like sitting down and crying, but I didn't. I just kept working through the anxiety and tension. I knew if we didn't pull this together, we would have an angry customer who could cancel his order. We all worked that weekend and a few late nights, but we were able to get the project done on time."

I think the strongest answer is _____.

ANSWERS

The Strongest Answer

(A) This is the strongest answer because it provides a specific example of how this candidate works in a fast-paced environment. This answer also conveys many other skills such as good communication skills, taking the initiative, coordinating projects, and managing time in an efficient manner. You could probe to get more information about any of the skills mentioned to get isolated examples of each trait. Try asking, "What was the largest project you ever coordinated? Tell me about it."

This answer also has a strong theme of doing above and beyond what was called for and doing whatever it takes to get the job done. These traits are to be valued in an employee because they are skills that cannot be taught.

The Mediocre Answer

(C) Although this answer gives an example of "a time when," it fails to provide any details that would demonstrate the individual's skills or explain the contribution this person made. With a few probes you could walk the candidate through this example and get the information that you need. Try asking, "Where specifically were you working when this happened?" or "What was your role in the project?"

The Weakest Answer

(B) This candidate states some skills that are good to possess, but she doesn't share anything specific. Note that this answer does share some redeeming traits worth following up on, such as being "involved in as many as 10 projects at the same time." Another statement to possibly probe more deeply into is, "I've never had an assignment on which I haven't been able to meet the deadline." Make sure that there is some evidence to back up these great claims of performance under pressure.

RATE YOURSELF

If you chose answer **(A),** give yourself 5 points.

If you chose answer **(C),** give yourself 3 points.

If you chose answer **(B),** give yourself 0 points. _____

INTERVIEWER'S QUESTION

42. Tell me about a time when you went above and beyond what the job required.

Which response actually answers the question? Which answer should you be wary of? Are there any red flags?

(A) "I have always been taught that 'time is money' and to value it as such. I plan my day so that I know how much time each task will require. Because my time is so well organized, sometimes I have extra time in a day and will ask coworkers if they need help, or I work on something proactive. I know how to use my time so that I am not caught off guard. I go out of my way to do whatever it takes to get the job done. My last boss was a last-minute type of person, and there were many times when I had to get him out of tough situations."

(B) "I am a person who believes in planning ahead. I always have a good handle on my work and my priorities. I go out of my way if coworkers need assistance. In fact, I think I go above and beyond almost every day. I am very responsive to customers' needs and problems and make sure that I have satisfied their expectations. I always get excellent performance reviews. I think I am a very dedicated support person who can be depended on to do the job and give it my all."

(C) "When I worked for an insurance company I had to process claims. This was a fairly routine job that was more time consuming than anything else. One day I decided to think of a way to use the Internet to process the claims, thereby cutting out hours of moving paper around. I took the time to organize a system that could be used as a prototype. I showed it to my boss, and she thought it was a great idea. She immediately showed it to her boss and he encouraged me to take it to the next step. This turned out to save the company hundreds of dollars and the processors, like myself, about two hours each day. I was rewarded for my original thinking and efforts above and beyond my normal job."

I think the strongest answer is _____.

ANSWERS

The Strongest Answer

(C) This answer illustrates a great example of thinking outside the box, of doing something not in the job description, and of taking the initiative to do it. This person has the transferable skills that most employers are seeking. This, combined with her knowledge of the job itself, would make her a strong candidate to consider. Sometimes transferable traits can make up for a lack of job knowledge that can be learned through some training and on-the-job experience.

The Mediocre Answer

(B) This answer has all the makings of a good reply but misses the mark by not being specific. Although this person claims to be able to plan ahead and have a handle on the workload (abilities that are to be admired in any person, particularly in a support person), she doesn't give proof that she actually possesses these qualities. She tells how she is responsive to customer's needs and problems but doesn't give a good example of a time when she actually helped someone. The same is true with the statement about her coworkers and going out of her way to assist them. These claims need examples to back them up.

The Weakest Answer

(A) This answer has no focus. It wanders through many thoughts but never answers the question asked. The candidate starts out talking about time and money and then goes on to talk about helping coworkers without a specific example of going above and beyond.

    She gives an excellent reference to her boss being a "last-minute type of person" who she has had to get out of tough spots, but she does not provide an example of an actual time when she helped to get results.

RATE YOURSELF

If you chose answer **(C),** give yourself 5 points.

If you chose answer **(B),** give yourself 3 points.

If you chose answer **(A),** give yourself 0 points. _____.

INTERVIEWER'S QUESTION

43. Give me an example of a time when you helped motivate or develop a coworker or subordinate.

Which response actually answers the question? Which answer should you be wary of? Are there any red flags?

(A) "I helped a coworker who was struggling with his workload. I asked him if I could give him help with his back orders. As we started to talk, I found out that he was going through a divorce and that he hadn't attended the training program on the new computer system. He was trying to work it out on his own. I asked if he would agree to work through a few lunch hours so that I could help him catch up. We agreed on a plan, and for the next few weeks we met during our lunch hours to bring him up to speed. His productivity improved, and he was my friend for life after that situation."

(B) "As the manager of the customer service team, I have found that competition motivates employees and they have fun competing. I have tried this various times, and it works like a charm every time. I always have a cash reward for those who reach certain goals or plateaus. The morale in the department improves, and the camaraderie improves. It's a great motivator."

(C) "My coaching skills are my strength. I have coached several people inside and outside my department. One rule I have is that they must try to help themselves first by making an extra effort. I can sense when someone is frustrated beyond the point of self-help, and I will try to work with him or her at that point. I don't believe in holding someone's hand, but I will help if someone is willing to try. Employees know that they can come to me for answers, and as a result they seek me out."

I think the strongest answer is _____.

ANSWERS

The Strongest Answer

(A) This is the strongest example and therefore the strongest answer to the question. The answer is specific and provides the
steps this candidate took to help another person with a problem. It also shows that this candidate is willing to go above and
beyond her regular duties by giving up lunch hours to help a
coworker. This is an indicator of a real team player. The fact that
she initiated the help and then volunteered to do something
about the problem is an indicator of caring as well as of her having the ability to be patient in teaching new things. More questions and probing will reveal whether there is a pattern of this
type of behavior or if this was an isolated incident.

The Mediocre Answer

(B) This is an okay answer because it tells you something about
the candidate; nevertheless, it does not answer the question.
The candidate has learned through experience what worked
well. In other words, he did it before, and he can do it again at
your company in this position. In order to get a specific answer
and the details of how the competition worked, you will need
to probe for more information, with questions like, "What
types of rewards were offered to the high achievers?"

The Weakest Answer

(C) This answer lack specifics. On the surface it sounds very good.
This candidate sounds like she has a real gift for seeking out and
helping people with problems. Yet there is a potential red flag.
You don't know if helping people is a part of this person's job responsibilities and, if not, how capable she is of handling her own
job responsibilities. In addition, if she is coaching people outside
her department, has this candidate overstepped the boundaries?
If the job you are recruiting for includes a need for coaching
skills, then you should probe further for specific information.

RATE YOURSELF

If you chose answer **(A),** give yourself 5 points.

If you chose answer **(B),** give yourself 3 points.

If you chose answer **(C),** give yourself 0 points. _____

INTERVIEWER'S QUESTION

44. Changes seem to be a way of life in our industry. Give me an example of how you keep abreast of the latest news and trends.

Which response actually answers the question? Which answer should you be wary of? Are there any red flags?

(A) "I do a great deal of reading, especially magazine articles. Part of strategic planning is to envision what is next. My major job has been product enhancement and extensions of the business. I have to admit that I left a big part of new technology research to my team members. I believe it is impossible to be an expert in all areas, and I rely on others to fill me in. I see my job as the bottom line accountability that will create significant new and profitable business."

(B) "I embrace technology and am an advocate of how it is changing our world and the way we do business. I use all the standard applications available and have a solid understanding of the basics of technology for this industry. I attend meetings and conferences on a regular basis to hear what is happening in other companies. I also belong to the industry association and attend monthly meetings, and I network with other executives. In addition I read four newspapers, and I subscribe to online news blogs, which I find invaluable. I find one of my best resources is my internal IT department members. I meet with the leaders of the department on a weekly basis."

(C) "I tend to view technology as somewhat out of my area of expertise. I use the Internet for research, and of course I use e-mail, but beyond that I don't get involved in the day-to-day issues. I have remained savvy regarding the latest management systems software, but my primary goal has been to exceed revenue expectations. The IT function is managed by experts. I trust my managers and as a result can focus more on the marketing of product and the customer track. I set high standards for myself and my staff and feel that ethical conduct is one of the most essential factors in a person. I try to foster that."

I think the strongest answer is _____.

ANSWERS

The Strongest Answer

(B) Not only does this answer give specific examples, but it demonstrates an appreciation of thinking beyond what is current to a vision of what can be. This answer also demonstrates respect for the technical people and what they contribute to the bigger picture. The candidate sounds like someone who is involved in a professional community and who does a good job of networking with other companies and executives. He definitely has his finger on the pulse of what is going on.

The Mediocre Answer

(A) Although this answer demonstrates an understanding of the role of technology in business, it suggests passivity and does not reveal the business acumen necessary to be involved in broad business or technical and economic trends. More probing may reveal that this person does get involved more than this answer indicates. Consider asking, "Are there ways you stay current in addition to reading? Can you give me some examples of how that is helpful for you?"

The Weakest Answer

(C) This answer strays off course and ultimately doesn't address the question about staying "abreast of the latest news and trends." While it is important for people to be experts in their own fields, it is also necessary that they maintain some knowledge of the ever-changing technical world and how it will affect future sales.

   This answer also does not demonstrate a visionary perspective. You will need to ask further questions to find out if this person is relying on others to take the responsibility of reporting the latest news and trends. Depending on the responsibilities of this position, this could be a red flag. The management style has the sound of passivity, but on the other hand, it could simply demonstrate a hands-off management style.

RATE YOURSELF

If you chose answer **(B)**, give yourself 5 points.

If you chose answer **(A)**, give yourself 3 points.

If you chose answer **(C)**, give yourself 0 points. _____

INTERVIEWER'S QUESTION

45. You say that one of your strengths is follow-through. Can you give me an example of a time when your follow-through made a difference in your work?

Which response actually answers the question? Which answer should you be wary of? Are there any red flags?

(A) "My work ethic is that if I say that I am going to do something, I do it. The way I have carried out this ethic in my job is to make a list of things to follow through on. I wouldn't have survived without my lists. Between supervising people and keeping track of their projects, and my own projects to track, I couldn't do it without making lists. I put little reminders on everything so that I remember to follow through. It probably isn't very sophisticated, but this system works for me. I can't remember a time when I missed a follow-through on a project."

(B) "As a human resources supervisor I have to constantly follow through on details of projects for managers. It seems as though everything happens at one time. There are performance appraisals and raises, and last year we had a mandatory holiday break. The date for the salary increases to be submitted was two weeks earlier than usual. If you've worked with managers who dreaded completing performance reviews, you will know what I am talking about when I say it can be 'like pulling teeth.' I did everything short of offering money to the two managers who were behind in their schedule, but I ended up agreeing to help them by parceling out a few reviews at a time to get them completed."

(C) "As a pharmaceutical sales rep I remember an incident when a doctor wouldn't see me because he had a bad experience with my company in the past. My strategy was to get past the office manager. I befriended him because I would visit once a week and bring samples for a basket they kept on the desk. We talked each time I came in, and I found that we had a favorite sports team in common. One day the doctor walked in and the office manager introduced me to the doctor and told the doctor that I was a fan of the same team. The three of us began talking and connecting. Eventually the doctor agreed to talk to me about my products. I was able to sell to this doctor after a four-year standoff because I followed through."

I think the strongest answer is _____.

ANSWERS

The Strongest Answer

(C) This is the strongest answer because it is a very strong example of someone's follow-through skills. Persistence is part of this person's job, and he went about it in a very nonaggressive manner. If this person is going to work in a sales capacity and because follow-through is such an important trait for a salesperson, you would probably want to ask for more examples of making a sale when there was an obstacle. Also note that in this answer there is an indication that this person has strong communication skills and the ability to build relationships, which are two key strengths needed for anyone dealing with customers.

The Mediocre Answer

(B) This answer focuses more on meeting a deadline than it does on the importance of follow-through. Because there are other skills described, probing may bring out the specific details of how follow-through and communication helped this candidate meet her deadline. Follow up by asking, "What steps did you take—short of offering them money—that worked so well in getting the performance appraisals on time? How did follow-through play a part in your success?"

The Weakest Answer

(A) Although this person seems to get things done, this is the weakest answer because it doesn't reveal much about the candidate and his successes except for the fact that he relies heavily on his "lists." Nevertheless, take note that he seems to have a strong work ethic and also appears to do what he says he is going to do. You will need to probe this candidate to learn more about his statement that he never missed a follow-through on a project. That alone could be worth your finding out if this is the right person for the type of work you are expecting him to do.

RATE YOURSELF

If you chose answer **(C)**, give yourself 5 points.

If you chose answer **(B)**, give yourself 3 points.

If you chose answer **(A)**, give yourself 0 points. _____

INTERVIEWER'S QUESTION

46. Give me an example of a time when you made a mistake related to your work.

Which response actually answers the question? Which answer should you be wary of? Are there any red flags?

(A) "This was a painful lesson for me. It was when I misquoted a price to the customer. Unfortunately, my company had to stand by my quote, and that cost it some money. I didn't get fired, but I did get a reprimand. That was a mistake that I will not make again. I always double-check now."

(B) "I'm not perfect, and have made mistakes in my career. But I don't dwell on mistakes. I learn from the incident and move on. Fortunately, none of my mistakes have been that big or cost the company any money."

(C) "I was a restaurant manager, and it was my responsibility to estimate and order supplies. There was an incident when I forgot about a local celebration that affected our business. When I saw we were going to run out of ingredients for main dishes, I drove to the local market and purchased the goods. Because I had such a great staff, we were able to pull together and work hard. We were tired but did not lose a single customer and I learned a lesson about planning ahead."

I think the strongest answer is _____.

ANSWERS

The Strongest Answer

(C) This answer provides a good example that explains the situation and then goes on to explain the action this candidate took in order to solve the problem. From the action steps in this answer, it's clear that this candidate can act quickly in a tight situation, work well with a team, and take responsibility for actions that caused a problem. In other words, this person was able to learn from his mistake.

The Mediocre Answer

(A) Although this answer gives a specific example, there are no details. If the company stood behind the price quoted, there must have been some discussion about the incident. Also, the candidate states that he "did not get fired," so you will have to probe to find out if there was policy violated or ignored to make this a serious problem. Some of the probes you might use are:

- What did you do when you discovered that you had misquoted the price?

- Did you have to deal with an angry customer?

- Was a policy or procedure violated?

The Weakest Answer

(B) This is the weakest answer because although the candidate says the right words about "not dwelling on mistakes," there are no specific examples given. This could be a possible red flag because you do not know if the mistakes were frequent or what they involved. It will be necessary to probe or to restate the question. Try asking, "Could you give me a specific example of a mistake you made and how often you made the same mistake?"

RATE YOURSELF

If you chose answer **(C)**, give yourself 5 points.

If you chose answer **(A)**, give yourself 3 points.

If you chose answer **(B)**, give yourself 0 points. _____

INTERVIEWER'S QUESTION

47. Describe a situation in which you had a difficult time meeting a deadline.

Which response actually answers the question? Which answer should you be wary of? Are there any red flags?

(A) "When I was in college, I had a part-time job. It was at the end of the semester, and I had finals to study for and a big paper due. The first thing I did was ask my boss if I could cut back on my hours if I made them up later. Then I put together a study group with other students in the class. I worked on my paper in chunks of two hours a day. I have to admit I was short on sleep during this period, but I received an A in the class and turned my paper in on schedule."

(B) "I was a project manager on a job, and one of the members of my group had a family emergency and had to travel leaving us short-handed. We had this project that was really important to the CEO, and we knew we had to pick up the slack. We all worked really hard with some late nights. We came close to missing the deadline, but we were able to get the job done on time. The CEO said we did a great job and thanked us all personally."

(C) "I can't remember a project that I had at my current job when we didn't have a tight deadline. That's the name of the game at this company. After two years of working in that mode, I wouldn't have any problem meeting deadlines no matter how tight they were."

I think the strongest answer is _____.

ANSWERS

The Strongest Answer

(A) This answer provides a specific example of how this candidate handles stress and knows how to negotiate as well as his ability to work collaboratively, plan, and "do whatever it takes" to get the job done. Since this is example is from this person's time in college, you may want to ask additional questions to learn about this person's professional experience with planning and meeting deadlines to determine if there is a pattern that has continued beyond school.

The Mediocre Answer

(B) This almost answers the question but offers no specifics or details. This example also has many "we's" and doesn't explain the candidate's individual role. It is acceptable for a candidate to talk about a group project and use the pronoun "we," but you will have to probe to find out what part of "we" the candidate played. Since this example begins with the candidate saying he was the project manager, the candidate does not give a good example of leadership and delegation.

The Weakest Answer

(C) This is the weakest answer because it is not specific, and also it has some potential red flags. After two years of tight deadlines this candidate could be experiencing burnout and is leaving his current job because he can't take the pressure any longer.

While this is a legitimate reason for wanting to leave a job, you will want to learn more about the circumstances around the reason the candidate is leaving at this particular time. This answer could have a negative connotation about the current job and employer. More probing questions may uncover more complaints. Candidates who talk negatively about their current or past employer may not be using discretion or good judgment. You will have to judge just how much complaining is done and how appropriate it is to the situation.

RATE YOURSELF

If you chose answer **(A)**, give yourself 5 points.

If you chose answer **(B)**, give yourself 3 points.

If you chose answer **(C)**, give yourself 0 points. _____

INTERVIEWER'S QUESTION

48. Tell me about a time when you negotiated a deal at your job.

Which response actually answers the question? Which answer should you be wary of? Are there any red flags?

(A) "The most stressful negotiation contract I had was when I was involved in purchasing and I had to deal with a shipping company and the price of shipping. The situation involved the materials we were shipping and the price we were being charged. I was able to work with the company representative to come to a mutually acceptable agreement. Even though we were slightly below the volume minimum needed to get a discount on the shipping, we agreed on a way that it was a win-win situation for all concerned."

(B) "As an administrative assistant, negotiations are not a normal part of my day-to-day duties, but we had been having problems with our coffee and the vendor wasn't responding to my calls. I was able to catch the vendor in person one day when he came in for a service call. I took the opportunity to tell him that we were very dissatisfied with the quality of the coffee as well as the service. He started to talk defensively in the beginning but eventually agreed that there was a problem. I spent time listening to what he had to say and treated him professionally. I told him that although I could hear the problems he was having, unless things improved, we would be forced to change accounts. He was eager to keep the account, so he and I negotiated better terms and he agreed to an upgrade in the coffee. My boss was very impressed with the way I handled the problem."

(C) "As buyer, my main focus is to evaluate any purchases the company makes and to shop around for the best terms and deals available. I was able to save the company $10,000 one year by discovering a better provider who could supply the same products at a much lower rate."

I think the strongest answer is _____.

ANSWERS

The Strongest Answer

(B) This is the strongest answer because it shows when the candidate actually negotiated a deal. It also shows how this person is good at taking the initiative. A candidate can say that he or she takes the initiative, but this example shows specific actions this candidate actually took. The fact that she treated the vendor with a professional demeanor and listened to him says a lot about the candidate. The outcome was positive in this case, but there doesn't always have to be a "happy ending." The best results have to do with the candidate's behavior and actions and not necessarily the financial gain.

The Mediocre Answer

(A) This is a mediocre answer because although the candidate gives the specifics of the situation and even the end results, there are no details about the actual method the candidate used to negotiate the deal. You will have to probe to find out more information. Consider asking:

- Did you initiate the negotiation to get a better deal?

- How much did you save the company in comparison to what it was paying before your negotiation?

The Weakest Answer

(C) This answer is the weakest answer although it does have some interesting facts that could require further probing. The question asks for a specific example of a negotiation. This answer tells of a savings of $10,000 over a year, but it does not tell how the person used her negotiation skills to save this much money. In other words, did the company have to agree with any terms in order to get bigger discounts? Was there a volume agreement, or did the company just offer better prices?

RATE YOURSELF

If you chose answer **(B)**, give yourself 5 points.

If you chose answer **(A)**, give yourself 3 points.

If you chose answer **(C)**, give yourself 0 points. _____

INTERVIEWER'S QUESTION

49. Tell me about a time when you worked collaboratively with a team.

Which response actually answers the question? Which answer should you be wary of? Are there any red flags?

(A) "I headed up a project on ways to improve customer service. The first thing I did was to organize a meeting with everyone involved to get ideas on improving satisfaction. I put all our ideas on a spreadsheet, and in a follow-up meeting we discussed which ideas were more important to incorporate short term and which were longer-term improvements. It was a very collaborative effort with me making sure things went smoothly. When we put the ideas into action, participants had a sense that they played a part in achieving the wonderful results. I received many compliments for pulling the team together."

(B) "One thing that I learned early in my career was that no one person makes a project successful. I have been the lead several times, but it is the individual team members who carry out and implement the ideas. My strong communication and organizational skills keep the project on track and moving forward. I can make the project move forward, but the team helps the project become successful."

(C) "Each member of the team plays a part in the success of a project. You have to encourage each person to stay focused on the 'whole project' whether it's a customer's needs or a long-term goal. And you have to recognize the individual team member's contribution. Communication skills are the key to successfully managing teams. Staying in touch with team members is vital to the idea of collaboration."

I think the strongest answer is _____.

ANSWERS

The Strongest Answer

(A) This is the strongest answer because it specifically shows how this person worked collaboratively with a team. He gives credit to each team member for his or her contribution; at the same time, the candidate's role is defined. When candidates tell stories about working collaboratively, they tend to use the pronoun "we" without defining their own roles. If they do use the pronoun "we" by itself, you will need to probe as to what role they played. That is not the case in this example.

The Mediocre Answer

(B) Although this answer shares the same ideas as the strongest answer, there are no details. The candidate claims to have been the lead several times but does not give an example of any project in particular. The candidate presents nice ideas by sharing her belief that "no one person makes a project successful," but because there are no specific examples, there is no way to determine if this person is being genuine. A possible follow-up probe is: "Could you be more specific about a particular project when you have worked with individuals who came together as a team?"

The Weakest Answer

(C) This answer provides only empty theories with no mention of the candidate's experience. He uses the pronoun "you" where he should be using "I." Some candidates will have a difficult time using the pronoun "I." They feel that they are taking too much credit and bragging. This could be a red flag, indicating that this person lacks confidence. To better judge what this candidate's experiences have been, try asking, "You say you believe in recognizing individual efforts. Could you give me an example of a time when you actually did that and what you did?"

RATE YOURSELF

If you chose answer **(A),** give yourself 5 points.

If you chose answer **(B),** give yourself 3 points.

If you chose answer **(C),** give yourself 0 points. _____

INTERVIEWER'S QUESTION

50. Describe a situation in which you influenced someone else's decision.

Which response actually answers the question? Which answer should you be wary of? Are there any red flags?

(A) "I am often the contact during labor negotiations and contract disputes. As the leader, I am able to let people on the opposing side know that I have heard the issues. I also let them know we are trying to accomplish a compromise. If both sides see that I am being open, we can talk it out to satisfy everyone involved. I find the key to successful communications is to look at the problem from the other person's point of view."

(B) "I am an experienced presenter and often make presentations to groups of major decision makers on their investments. I am an excellent presenter and have had a good deal of positive feedback on my ability to make my point and can usually influence decisions. I think part of my success is that I enjoy giving presentations and feel that I really connect with my audience."

(C) "I had a customer who didn't think he needed a particular product and did not want to buy. He told me he would listen to my product presentation because he liked me. I began by showing an interest in what he did and his plans for future growth. By listening carefully, I saw a way that my product could greatly assist him in reaching his future goal. I spent time with him on multiple visits to show him how I understood his need. In the end I received a nice order and made a long-lasting relationship."

I think the strongest answer is _____.

ANSWERS

The Strongest Answer

(C) This is the strongest answer because it gives a great deal of specific information. It provides a good example of how the candidate used a sales technique that involved listening skills which is important in qualifying a customer's needs. Other skills that are mentioned are determination and the ability to follow up, which are important skills for anyone in a position that requires relationship building.

The answer also indicates this is a likeable person who even builds relationships with a customer who did not intend to buy from him. Further questions regarding customer relationships and successful results through communication will determine if this is a pattern of behavior or a single success story.

The Mediocre Answer

(A) This answer gives only a sample of a technique used to influence without the specifics of an actual success. In order to find out if this person is all bark and no bite, you will need more information about his communication technique. Try to find out if he is capable of listening to both sides without being influenced by one or the other. To learn more about this person's behavior, try asking, "Could you describe a situation in which you arrived at a compromise that both sides felt were good?"

The Weakest Answer

(B) This answer is weak, not because of the answer itself but because it does not give a concrete example of winning over the major decision makers. The candidate claims she has the "ability to make my point and to influence decisions." Even if this person is the best candidate, she has presented her information without facts to back her claim. By asking more questions and probing further, you can determine if she has the skills that you are seeking in a candidate.

RATE YOURSELF

If you chose answer **(C)**, give yourself 5 points.

If you chose answer **(A)**, give yourself 3 points.

If you chose answer **(B)**, give yourself 0 points. _____

Review of Questions:
Point Evaluation

After each item indicate your score in points in the blank provided.

1. Learning about a candidate's background and experience. _____
2. Determining what a candidate has to offer that the other candidates don't have. _____
3. Learning if a candidate has what it takes to do the job. _____
4. Determining if you have a personality fit. _____
5. Determining a candidate's motivation. _____
6. Learning about potential problems that could affect performance. _____
7. Learning about how a candidate gets along with others. _____
8. Understanding how candidates cope with failure. _____
9. Determining someone's ability to learn from mistakes. _____
10. Probing for something missing or hidden in the candidate's experience. _____
11. Determining which accomplishments the candidate is proudest of. _____
12. Talking about the candidate's strengths. _____
13. Learning about candidates' experience with working in teams and groups. _____
14. Learning what the candidate's biggest challenge would be if he or she got this job. _____
15. Determining particular areas of expertise. _____
16. Ascertaining the candidate's communication skills. _____
17. Determining the candidate's attention to detail. _____
18. Assessing the candidate's organizational skills. _____
19. Rating someone's problem-solving skills. _____
20. Learning how candidates work with others. _____
21. Learning a candidate's preferred work situation. _____
22. Uncovering a candidate's goals. _____
23. Determining how long someone will stay with your company. _____
24. Learning why the applicant wants to work for your company. _____

25. Determining why someone left, or is leaving, his or her last position. _____

26. Tell me about a time when you solved a problem by thinking creatively. _____

27. Describe a time when you had to adapt to a new situation. _____

28. Can you give me an example of a time when you were working on a project that required sustained and persistent effort? _____

29. Would you give me an example of a time when you worked on a project that required a great deal of written communication? _____

30. Tell me about a time when you used strategic thinking to solve a problem. _____

31. You say you have good customer service skills. Tell me about a time when you dealt with an angry customer. _____

32. Describe a time when you had to make an unpopular decision. _____

33. Tell me about a time when you took the initiative concerning something that you saw needed to be done. _____

34. Give me an example of an obstacle you faced and how you overcame it. _____

35. Can you give me an example of a time when your leadership made a difference in your current or previous job? _____

36. Describe your experience working with global markets by giving me an example of a project you worked on. _____

37. Tell me about a time when you had a conflict with a boss or coworker. _____

38. Tell me about the biggest project you worked on from start to finish. _____

39. Tell me about a time when you had to convince someone to do something that he or she did not want to do. _____

40. You say you have good customer service skills. Tell me about a time when your customer service skills helped you in a difficult situation. _____

41. Give me an example of your working in a fast-paced environment. _____

42. Tell me about a time when you went above and beyond what the job required. _____

43. Give me an example of a time when you helped motivate or
develop a coworker or subordinate. _____

44. Changes seem to be a way of life in our industry. Give me
an example of how you keep abreast of the latest news
and trends. _____

45. You say that one of your strengths is follow-through.
Can you give me an example of a time when your
follow-through made a difference in your work? _____

46. Give me an example of a time when you made a mistake
related to your work. _____

47. Describe a situation in which you had a difficult time
meeting a deadline. _____

48. Tell me about a time when you negotiated a deal at
your job. _____

49. Tell me about a time when you worked collaboratively
with a team. _____

50. Describe a situation in which you influenced someone
else's decision. _____

RATE YOURSELF: POINT EVALUATION

Count up your points. Where do you stand as an interviewer? Evaluate your total points as follows, using the Interview Ability Rating Point System:

- **176–250 points: savvy interviewer**

You've got the idea. Now use your technique to prepare for your next interview. Apply your own key factors and rating system to find the *right* person for the job.

- **100–175 points: above-average interviewer**

Being aware of what you are looking for and what the key factors of the job are will greatly increase your savvy. Preparing the answers before the interview will also give you the increased knowledge you will need to judge this candidate against the other candidates.

- **Below 100 points: average interviewer**

This does not mean that you are a bad interviewer, but it could indicate that you need to think more about the process before you begin to select people without first having a plan. Some analysis of what you need on various levels will help you form your wish list or requirements for the job. This will aid you significantly in selecting people who are well suited to the job in all areas.

PART 2

The Surefire Way to Boost Your Score

The Planning Stage

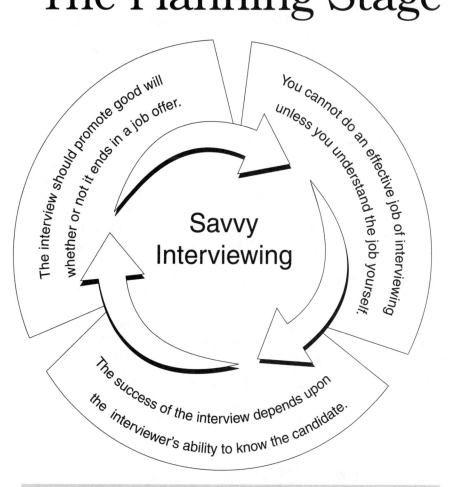

The interview should promote good will whether or not it ends in a job offer.

You cannot do an effective job of interviewing unless you understand the job yourself.

Savvy Interviewing

The success of the interview depends upon the interviewer's ability to know the candidate.

You cannot do an effective job of interviewing unless you understand the job yourself.

If you have ever had to hire anyone, then the following is likely a very familiar scenario:

> *James gives notice to his boss that he will be leaving in two weeks. The boss, Bob, picks up the phone and calls human resources to relay the news and to request that the process of replacing James be started.*
>
> *The human resources administrator goes to James's file and pulls out a copy of the job description and the ad used to hire James 3½ years ago. The ad is posted on the Internet, and perhaps a recruiter is called and given the information. The process moves forward to the next step.*

Before the Interview Begins

If the above scenario is the approach your company uses to hire and replace personnel, perhaps it is time for an overhaul of your hiring system. Often hiring is done with little more than a passing thought about what has changed in the job since the last time the job was open. Instead of following this routine, when a new hiring situation occurs, take the opportunity to identify your specific needs and to improve on the hiring process.

Whether you have a human resources department in your company or not, some basic planning before you place a posting or begin to interview candidates will save you and your company valuable time and money.

First, it's important to know what you are looking for. Assessing the candidate's ability can be done only if the interviewer knows what he or she is seeking. To do a good job of interviewing, a careful analysis of the position and the requirements of the job should be conducted. Next, the appropriate questions should be prepared before the interview begins to make the process as effective as possible. By taking these preliminary steps, many costly hiring mistakes can be avoided.

Understanding the Job and the Role to Be Filled

Here are some basic questions to ask before the hiring process begins:

- Why do you need someone for this job?

- If you are replacing someone, did the person who held the job fill the position the way it was intended to be filled? What qualities was he or she lacking?

- Are there new requirements that would improve efficiency?

- Is it possible to restructure the functions performed in this position?

- Could the functions be split or combined with another position?

In other words, are you gaining something by filling this position in exactly the same way it was filled before? Or can you benefit by analyzing what has been done in the past to determine whether any changes should be made at this time?

It is important to be as specific and as detailed as possible in defining the position's functions. By taking time to write a thorough list of the responsibilities, you will find that you can use the information later to write the job description, the ad, or posting and that you may even be able to use the information for compliance with the American with Disabilities Act (ADA), which requires you to define the essential and marginal duties as well as the responsibilities of each job.

Identifying Required Skills— The Three Categories

One common mistake that many interviewers make is to hire someone because of that person's knowledge-based skills.

> *Knowledge-based skills*—Skills learned through experience or education. Examples are computer programming, graphics, languages, writing, training, management, chemistry, coaching, sales, and leadership.

Knowledge-based skills certainly play an important role in the candidate's ability to perform the duties of the job, such as the ability to speak another language or have a specific technical background, and maybe possess some other special knowledge or degree. It is, however, a mistake to focus entirely on these skills and ignore other factors. To make a truly strong hiring decision, you must have a complete picture of your candidates, and that includes asking questions to learn about their transferable skills and personal traits.

These other skills are often referred to as the *soft skills*. But very often it is these skills that turn out to be the most important part of the job performance.

Sometimes the right person has a great attitude and strong abilities in communication, flexibility, problem solving, and interpersonal skills, but lacks some of the requirements of the job. You might want to take a good look at this person before you cross him or her off your list. Consider first whether this person can be taught some of the knowledge-based skills. It is not uncommon for a hiring manager to say, "Find me the right person, and we will train that person for the position."

Transferable skills—Skills that are portable and can be used on almost any job. Examples include communication, listening ability, decision-making ability, judgment, initiative, negotiation, planning, organizing, time management, and some leadership skills.

Not to be overlooked are candidates' personal traits. These are those characteristics that make them unique, or who they are. Even though employers would like to change these skills in some people, they really can't easily be taught. A person's personal traits are inherent or acquired through life experiences.

When making hiring decisions, two important questions to ask are

1. Can he do the job?

2. Do we like her; will she fit in?

Personal traits can sometimes be the tiebreaker between two equally qualified candidates.

Personal traits: Qualities that make up a person's personality. These include flexibility, integrity, friendliness, dependability, decisiveness, reliability, calmness, high energy, patience, good attitude, adaptability, and orientation to details.

Only by looking at all three skill sets will you have a full and accurate picture of the candidate and how he or she will fit in and perform in your company's culture and environment.

The Key Factors Necessary

The next step is to determine the key factors of the job. Your task is to identify the key skills or competencies necessary to do this job. Identifying key factors will define the focus of the skills you are seeking in a candidate and will determine the questions you will ask.

Here is an example of a key factor analysis:

1. Start with the responsibilities. For example, "Develop and maintain supplier relationships at the property and chain levels through daily contact."

2. Identify skills needed by asking, "What would it take to perform this job?" Here are some examples:

- *Good communication skills.*

- *Listening skills.*

- *Ability to build customer relations.*

- *Follow-through.*

- *Tracking.*

- *Organizational skills.*

- *Ability to work with a wide variety of people.*

By reading through the responsibilities on your job description and writing down the skills you think would be needed under each category, you will be able to define those key factors. You can then narrow the list down to five or six key factors to be used in the interview process.

Beyond the Job Description

When you read through the job description and determine the key factors, you will have the tools necessary to assess your candidate—almost. But before you finalize your job description, it is beneficial to take some time to determine on your own or through a discussion with other people who will interact with this candidate what it "really" takes to do this job.

The success of the interview depends upon the interviewer's ability to get to know an applicant.

In other words, consider the transferable skills and personal traits that will be necessary for this person to have in order to succeed in your company's culture and environment and as a team member of your existing staff.

Preferred Personality Type

While you should have a flexible attitude about the person you are about to hire, be careful to not stereotype or have a prejudice against one type of personality or another. And remember that some jobs will require more of certain skills than will other jobs.

For example, it is hard to imagine a shy or withdrawn person being very satisfied or effective as a salesperson. On the other hand, a person who is a "people person" stuck away in a back room with no interaction with people all day would be unlikely to find job satisfaction.

Because a great deal of the interview process is matching personalities with the job, it is important to look at the responsibilities of the job and determine the type of personality that will be the best fit for the position. If the interview process is looked at objectively, the idea is to find a win-win situation for the candidate and for the company.

Following are some examples of factors for success needed in specific jobs:

- *Cognitive skills:* The intellectual ability and capacity to reason, think logically, and use good business judgment.

- *Administrative skills:* An ability to structure work, plan ahead, and develop action plans to achieve an objective.

- *Communication skills:* The ability to write and think effectively. These skills include the spoken work in personal settings, with groups, and in formal presentations.

- *Interpersonal skills:* These relate to a person's style of dealing with people and include creating goodwill and establishing relationships. These also include a sensitivity and understanding of others. These skills are key to people in leadership roles.

- *Personal motivation:* A desire to get ahead and work hard. This also suggests a high work ethic and drive and energy. This is also a key skill in a leadership role.

- *Adaptability:* Flexibility and emotional stability as well as the capability for readily accepting change.

- *Occupational/technical knowledge:* The knowledge and skills related to the requirements of the job.

When a person is satisfied in a job, he or she will be more motivated than someone who is not satisfied. A more motivated person will perform better. So it makes sense to try to find people who will satisfy your requirements while at the same time satisfying their own needs..

Forms and Tools

After you have a sense of what type of person you want to hire, it's important to have a system for measuring how closely a candidate fits your needs. The tools and forms you can use to rate the candidate will vary according to the size of your company. For example, you can use anything from a sophisticated printed form to a simple checklist to even a blank piece of paper.

The importance of whatever tool you use is that it will enable you to organize your thoughts before, during, and after the interview. Take notes during the interview in order to remember the specific words the candidate used, whether they impress you or if they seem like a possible red flag.

Using some type of form will assist you in keeping your interview on track and ensure that the conversations you have with each candidate are consistent. If you have nothing else, you can use the following simple five-point rating system:

1 = Much less than acceptable.

2 = Less than acceptable.

3 = Acceptable (qualified).

4 = More than acceptable.

5 = Much more than acceptable.

Use this basic rating system with your five or six identified factors (i.e., communications, interpersonal skills, decision-making skills, leadership, problem-solving skills, etc.). Assigning specific numbers will allow you to take an objective approach in your decision making rather than a personal or subjective approach.

If several people are going to interview the same candidate, it is important that the form be consistent for all interviewers so that when you get together to compare, you are all reading from the same page.

Preparing the Questions

If you prepare a list of questions you want to ask each candidate, you will find the interview to be less stressful for you and more conversational with better results. Preselecting questions for the interview and preparing a list of key questions will provide you with a guide to follow as you conduct the interview.

Each interview will be different, depending on the circumstances and personality of the candidate and will require some flexibility on your part as the interviewer. If you prepare before the interview, you can stay consistent with your questions even though the interview and circumstances may vary.

Organizing Your Interview Questions

While there are some key factors that are broad enough to be a requirement in every job, there are also be factors that are be relevent only to specific positions. When organizing your questions, you should start with general questions and then move into more specific areas.

General Questions—All Industries
The most used general questions are

- Tell me about yourself.
- What are your strengths?
- What are your weaknesses?
- Give me a good reason that we should hire you?
- What makes you think that you want to work here?
- What are your goals?

- What was the reason that you left (are you leaving) your job?

- When were you most satisfied in your job?

- What can you do for us that other candidates can't?

- What salary are you seeking?

Position Questions—Specific Positions

Moving beyond the basic, introductory questions to the more specific position questions is necessary to find out if the person has the skills to succeed in the position (unless, of course, it is an entry-level position).

You can use the job description to formulate these specific questions. If, for instance, the position is a sales job, you might ask one of the following questions:

- What was the most difficult product you've had to sell?

- Give me an example of you successfully selling this product to a customer.

Of, if you are hiring for an administrative position, you might ask

- Have you worked with people who gave you assignments without giving complete instructions?

- Could you give me a recent example of how you handled that situation?

An example of a question you could ask someone interviewing for a supervisory or management position might be "Tell me about the last time you were responsible for organizing a project and supervising the work of others."

You can see that the above questions probe for specific information about behavior in past situations. These can be the source of valuable information.

Self-Evaluation/Preference Questions

Self-evaluation questions can be very telling because most candidates haven't prepared for them. These are questions in which the candidates rate themselves or describe how they think others see them.

Good examples of self-evaluation and preference questions are

- On a scale of 1 to 10, how would you rate yourself in this field?

- If I were to ask your coworkers to describe you to me, what would they tell me?

- What is your strength? What is your weakness?
- What is your preference—working alone or working with a team?
- Would you rather lead a team or be a member of a team?

This type of questioning may reveal a great deal about candidates and their preferences as well as their confidence level.

Motivational Questions

Motivational questions allow you to determine if a candidate will be satisfied in the position. One way to find out about someone's satisfaction level is to ask about when he or she was most satisfied or dissatisfied in previous jobs. When you find out when the candidate was most satisfied, then you can probe further to find out what created the satisfaction in that job. For example, you can ask, "What motivated you the most at your previous job? Was it the people? The culture? The job responsibilities? The paycheck?"

Listen to the answers to determine if your position and company culture will be a good fit for the candidates given their previous experiences. If they were dissatisfied at a job that is very similar to your job, what makes you think that they won't be dissatisfied at your company, doing this job? This should be considered a red flag and will need further investigation.

Illegal Questions

It's important to know what questions you cannot ask because of legal restrictions. There are actually questions that are illegal and improper to ask. A good rule of thumb to be on the safe side is to ask only job-related questions. If the question strays from the specifics of the job, you begin to get into dangerous waters.

Stay away from any topic that focuses on personal information. You should not ask about age, marital status, number of children, religion, politics, or place of origin. If a candidate volunteers the information, be sure to note that in your record of the interview.

All candidates should receive fair and equal treatment, whatever your procedure. An example of perceived discrimination was when a woman over the age of 50 claimed age discrimination because she was not given an application to fill out the way the other candidates were. Make sure that if candidates are required to fill out an application, each person is given an application. This is a necessary step to prevent someone from claiming unfair treatment.

Discrimination can be categorized under the following categories:

- Race and color discrimination
- Religious discrimination
- Sex (gender) discrimination
- Sexual orientation discrimination
- Age discrimination
- Discrimination of disabled persons

The Seven Most Common Mistakes Interviewers Make

Following are the seven mistakes most commonly made by interviewers:

1. *Judging a book by its cover:* First impressions can be very deceiving. Impressions made in the first five minutes of an interview can cloud your judgment if you don't keep an open mind. This type of snap decision about a person can work for or against the candidate—with the same disastrous results.

2. *"Winging" the interview:* When you have not done your prep work before the interview and have not studied the résumé or at least skimmed the résumé, you are shortchanging the candidate as well as your employer. Preparing the questions and determining in advance the factors that are key to the job will make a significant difference in the outcome of your selection process.

3. *Talking too much:* A good rule of thumb is to let the candidate talk 80 percent of the time while you talk only 20 percent of the time. A talkative interviewer does not get the information necessary to determine whether this candidate is the right candidate for the job. The process done properly is a two-way communication of questions and answers.

4. *Telegraphing the desired response:* Beware of giving the candidate the answer that you are looking for. An example would be, "You don't mind working extra hours, do you?" It's pretty obvious that the answer to that question is, or should be, no. When you lead candidates, you make it convenient for them to try to please you with the answers they think you are looking for instead of the real answer.

5. *Asking closed-ended questions:* When you ask questions that can be answered with a single word, you are not getting the information you need to make a judgment. An example of a closed-ended question is, "Have you ever presented to large groups?" A yes or no answer will require you to probe for more information to find out the experience the candidate has had presenting to large groups.

6. *Asking threatening questions:* "What was the *real* reason you left your last job?" or, "Why didn't you stay at your job longer?" are types of questions that can be threatening when asked in an interview. These questions affix blame on the candidate and imply that he or she did something wrong. They put the candidate on the defensive. When the candidate is put on the defensive, you create a barrier between the two of you, and everyone loses.

7. *Not controlling the interview:* It is up to you as the interviewer to be in control of the time and the climate of the interview. No interview should make the candidate feel intimidated or hostile toward you or your company. If you can be objective and realize that you will be talking to a number of people and some will be the type of candidate you are seeking and some will not, you will have a better chance of making an objective decision based on facts.

The selection process is a very important step in your company's future. When you fail to take the time to prepare for this important step, you are taking the chance that you may or may not succeed in choosing the best candidate.

In the following chapter you will learn more about the importance of handling the interview process in a professional, objective, and fair manner. The small amount of time you take to prepare today could affect your overall employee satisfaction and the turnover rate for a long time to come.

The Selection Process

As we did in Part I, let's look at a very familiar interview scenario:

John arrives 10 minutes before his interview appointment and announces himself to the receptionist. She is very cordial and asks him to have a seat while she locates the manager. In the meantime he is given an application to fill out. Fifteen minutes later John finishes the application and sits waiting for the interviewer. The receptionist informs John that it will be a few more minutes. As John sits waiting, he is able to watch the employees in the company as they walk through the lobby. Everyone seems in a hurry, and no one appears to be very happy. He can overhear a conversation in an adjacent office, and the voices sound stressed. After half an hour, he is told to go down the hall to the third door on the right. John is now concerned. He feels a cold chill. Is this the way they treat all candidates, or is this just a bad day?

Setting the Stage— Establishing the Environment

Any candidate is a potential customer, stockholder, or future employee and should be received as such. When you treat the candidate with disrespect, you are sending a clear message that he or she doesn't really count. This person may get the impression that this is the general attitude of the company toward its employees. Leaving the applicant sitting in the lobby for more than a few minutes may set a negative tone for the interview.

Schedule interview appointments so that you will be able to devote time and attention to the task. Remember that there is a lot of money being spent with each hiring decision—thousands of dollars, in fact. This is a time investment that is worth your full attention. Reserve an office, or conference room, with two chairs and a table or desk away from your regular office or workspace. Make sure that no phones will ring during the interview, unless there is an emergency. It is a rude practice of some interviewers to take calls in the middle of the interview. Conduct this interview as you would any other important business transaction.

Promoting Goodwill

Every person who comes to interview in your company has at least five or more friends who will hear about the experience, good or bad. If the person leaves with a bad impression or having had a bad experience, the word will spread quickly.

When you are told that the applicant has arrived or is filling out an application, ask to be notified when the candidate is ready. When you get the call, go out to greet your visitor with enthusiasm. A smile and a hearty handshake can do wonders to make a person feel welcome and invited. Pronounce your name distinctly, or hand the candidate your business card, to assist him or her in knowing who you are and the role that you play in the organization.

> The interview should promote goodwill between the candidate and the interviewer, regardless of whether or not it ends in a job offer.

Putting the Candidate at Ease

The majority of candidates, even those at the executive level, feel nervous about interviewing: sweaty hands, fluttery heart, or feelings of anxiety. In fact, you may feel nervous about the process yourself, especially if you are new to interviewing and making judgments and decisions about candidates. Nervousness is perfectly normal in this situation. It is probably equal to the feeling you may get when you're giving a presentation. Being prepared will give you a secure foundation and lessen your anxiety.

Begin by being a good host, making the candidates feel welcome and comfortable. Good manners dictate that the candidates will wait for you to indicate where to sit or will wait until you are seated. Put them at ease by asking them to sit down and indicating which chair is theirs. It is also courteous to offer a beverage. Water is usually welcome, since one of the typical symptoms of being nervous is dry mouth.

Take a few minutes to begin. Make some small talk, if you are comfortable doing that, about the driving directions, traffic, and the company in general. If you prefer, pick up on something on the candidate's résumé. "I see you worked over at EZY Company. I worked there some years ago," or, "We had a contract with that company a few years ago." The applicant will be pleased to know that you took some time to read the résumé and actually have something in common to discuss. Whatever your style, the idea is to try to break the ice and help the applicants to relax and feel comfortable; this ultimately will aid in their ability to answer questions more openly.

One man's description of his role as a candidate is "goalie at a hockey game—sending back pucks." The interview should be an active conversation from both sides of the desk to determine the candidate's fit within the organization. Make an effort to engage with the candidate by asking open-ended questions and by listening attentively to the responses.

Describing the Interview Procedure

The interview should be an exchange, a conversation. If there is a hostile or unfriendly feeling to the environment, you will not get an accurate reading of the candidate. Taking time to explain the procedure and what to expect will help alleviate some of the anxiety for the candidate. For example, say something like:

Before we begin I'd like to tell you about the process we use here and what you can expect today. I will interview you for about an hour. Then I'll take you to the human resources department, where you will be interviewed by our staffing representative, Jim Taylor. Jim will give you information about the company and tell you what the next steps in the process will be.

I will begin our interview by asking some general questions about you and your experience, and then I'll move to more specific questions about the job and your fit for the position.

I will be taking notes throughout the process. Please feel free to take notes as well and to ask questions as we move through the process. (If you would prefer, you can ask the candidate to hold questions until the end of the interview.) I will give you an opportunity to ask additional questions at the end of the interview. Do you have any questions before we begin?

Then explain the essential function of the job and ask the candidate if he or she can perform the duties of the job with reasonable accommodation. If possible, provide the candidate with a description of the job.

Taking Notes

Even if you have a photographic memory, you will need to take notes during the interview. Use the prepared form which we discussed in Step One, or a notepad. Notes should be taken consistently throughout the interview so that they will be less disruptive to the candidate. If you suddenly stop and write something down right after it is said, it may cause the candidate to wonder what mistake he or she just made.

Note taking requires some skill, since you will be listening to what is being said and also trying to get key points down on paper. It will become easier after you have done it a few times, and with experience, you will devise your own form of shorthand. The following provides an example scenario of note taking:

You are interviewing Marianne, and she gives you an example of her experience in leading a team of 40 people. After analyzing the processes used, she was able to initiate a $2 million cost-saving program through improvements in procedures and training. She received the "key player" award for the year. (This example demonstrates ability to lead, improve process, take initiative, analyze, and think outside the box as well as demonstrating cost-saving experience savvy and experience.)

Example of note taking: led team 40, analy skil, init project, $2M save—key player.—leader, initit, big picture, $.

Your notes will assist you in asking more specific questions and will prompt you to delve deeper into the answer using behavioral questions.

For example, in this situation, you might want to ask the following question to learn more about this specific candidate:

You said you led a team of 40 people. What types of positions did those people hold?

Taking notes will also help you stay on track and recall what was said after the candidate has gone. When you have interviewed several people in one day, it is easy to get the stories and the people mixed up. By taking good notes, you will be able to go back and review. Attach your notes to the candidate's résumé or application for future reference and so that they can serve as part of the record.

Use a clipboard or pad of paper with a cardboard backing so that you can hold your notes out of view of the candidates. (There is a temptation on the part of the candidates to try to see what you are writing about them.) This will allow you to write more openly.

Be aware that your notes become a form of record, if kept. In other words, make sure that there is nothing in the notes that could be considered illegal or discriminatory, like referring to someone as a "fat guy."

Beginning the Interview

Your preparation will now pay off as you begin the interview with a clear objective in mind. Bring your prepared list of questions or the form you put together based on key dimensions of the position. Begin by asking general, broad-based questions about background and previous experience. These questions will focus primarily on the person and where he or she has been.

The success of the interview depends on the interviewer's ability to learn about a candidate.

Most interviews begin with some version of the, "Tell me about yourself" statement. Let the candidates have free reign and see where they go with it. You may find that this is one of the most revealing answers you will receive during the interview.

Let's Begin by Having You Tell Me about Yourself and Your Background

Candidates may ask you where you would like them to start. This is their personal statement, and you should return the question by saying, "That's really up to you."

Listen to where they go next. Are they prepared with a statement? Is the statement memorized or natural? Do they exhibit confidence, or do they seem embarrassed to talk about themselves? Where do they focus their information? This will be an area for you to probe now or later.

Sometimes personal information will come out of this statement, which is illegal for you to ask about in an interview. Handle this carefully so that it cannot be claimed that you asked for this information.

Here's an example of volunteered information that you would not have asked for: *"I took time out from my career to spend time at home after the birth of my son."*

You now have some information about this candidate's personal life. She didn't have to tell you why she took the time off—to raise her child—but since she volunteered the information, you now know she has a small child. This may not be a problem for you—or, it could be a decisive factor in your decision whether to hire this woman over someone who does not have small children—because of concern about attendance.

It would be advisable to stay away from that subject of a young child and to focus on the job and whether she is a good match for the job.

I'd Like You to Walk Me through Your Résumé and the Responsibilities You've Had at Each of Your Jobs

In this review stage of the interview you should take the opportunity to ask the candidates to clarify vague words or terms they used to describe some of the responsibilities they had. For example:

- *Knowledge of*—read a book?
- *Handled*—walked it from one department to another?
- *Involved with*—just what kind of involvement?
- *Worked closely with*—worked in small attached cubicles?

In addition to reading and referring to the résumé and listening to what the candidates have to say, observe the body language and enthusiasm regarding past jobs. Where the candidate places the emphasis can give you an indication of when they were most motivated or did their best work.

Having the applicants walk you through their résumé will be a very rich source of information. It is worthwhile to spend 15 minutes or so of the one-hour interview on the résumé. It will give you a context to refer to when you begin to ask behavioral types of questions.

What Is Causing You to Consider Leaving Your Current Job or What Caused You to Leave Your Last Job?

There is usually a specific reason or event that prompts a person to leave a job. Many candidates will give you a textbook answer to this question such as one of the following:

- *Quit to find a more challenging job:* Candidates will talk about seeking a "greater challenge, where they can use their skills to the best of their ability." Try to find out exactly what all that means to them. Follow up with questions like, "What kind of a challenge are you looking for? What makes you think we can offer a more challenging job then their last employer did?" Do they really know what they are looking for, or are they simply applying at companies that have openings?

- *Laid off:* Many people have been laid off. How do they convey this information? Did they see the layoff coming and remain at their job because they were in denial? Were they proactive about the layoff? Did they see this as a necessary business decision? Are they part of a large reduction in force? Why them? Watch for signs of anger or the display of feelings of betrayal.

- *Fired:* Some candidates may have been fired. They may want to make it sound like it was their decision or the fault of someone else. In either case, be sure to probe for more detail. If it happened before, it could happen again. We've all made mistakes in life. Are they willing to take responsibility for their mistake? Probe to understand how they came out of the situation with questions like, "What did you learn from the experience?" or, "How would you handle that situation differently today?"

Sometimes candidates do not have much in the way of past work experience. If you are interviewing for an entry level position or are someone who has just graduated from school, this person will not have had a lot of experience to talk about. Ask questions about classes, projects, internships, part-time jobs, or volunteer work. As with every candidate, you are trying to get an idea of this person's past behavior, and under what circumstances he or she was motivated.

Listen with Interest

To exhibit good listening skills and to indicate to the candidate that you are interested in what he or she is saying, try the following techniques:

- *Reflecting back:* Make comments like, "It sounds like you had a difficult time in that position," or, "That must have been a very challenging project to undertake."

- *Nonverbal clues:* Leaning forward in your chair demonstrates interest. Leaning back in your chair is intimidating. Change your posture throughout the interview.

- *Keep your energy level up:* Just as you pick up or lose energy from the candidate, he or she will reflect your style. Many people are trained to mirror the interviewer's posture and attitude.

- *Acting enthusiastically:* Some candidates are more interesting than others, and sometimes showing enthusiasm will take an effort on your part, especially if the candidate has a monotone voice and is low key.

- *Encouragement:* Nodding your head occasionally is a sign to the candidate that you are listening and interested.

- *Keeping a poker face:* Even though you may be shocked at what is being said, show no surprise or distaste. When the applicant shares, "My last boss made sexual advances toward me, and I am in the process of bringing a sexual harassment suit," hold that expression—no raised eyebrows. This is not a time to judge or advise.

Identifying Behaviors and Patterns

The work you have done by determining the qualities you are looking for prior to the interview will help you identify those specific skills and traits you are seeking during the actual interview. You will see patterns begin to emerge, and you will know the hot areas or red flags to watch for. You are listening for past experiences that reveal the way each candidate has handled difficult situations.

At this point in the interview you will begin to have some insight into the candidate's communication style and whether or not this person is going to fit into your culture. This fit will be important to the candidate as well as to the company. The expense involved in recruiting will be wasted if the employee is unsatisfied with the job and leaves after only

Key general skills and traits to listen for:

- *Communication skills:* How was the language and communication style used by the candidate, for example, proper grammar or appropriate stories? Were the voice and tone confident?

- *Listening skills:* How well has the applicant been listening? Did she or he answer the question as asked?

- *Focus:* How prepared and informed is the candidate about your company and the industry?

- *Nonverbal skills:* What was the candidate's body language, posture, and eye contact like? Did he or she sit stiffly or appear natural and animated?

- *Energy level:* What were the levels of energy and enthusiasm? Was the candidate able to talk about his or her job with passion?

a few months. The ideal situation is to have a win-win situation for all concerned.

It is now time to get more specific about the job duties, and whether candidates have the experience and the skills to do the job. To uncover the story of their work history, ask behavioral-based questions. The answers to behavioral questions will give you an indication of what the candidates did before, somewhere else, and whether they are likely do it again. The answers they reveal can be either positive or negative.

Behavioral Interview Techniques

The behavioral interviewing technique allows employers to determine whether someone is a good fit for the job. One way to accomplish this is by asking questions that pertain to past behavior on the job. The information gained through this technique is used as an indicator of the candidate's future success. In other words, the answers someone gives about his or her past experiences will be used to predict future performance.

This is not a new technique; it's been around since the 1970s when industrial psychologists developed a way of "accurately" predicting whether a person would succeed in a job. They concluded that if candidates were asked questions that requested examples of past behavior, it would be an indicator of their future behavior. The difference between a behavioral question and other questions is that a behavioral question asks for a very specific answer. An example would be, "Tell me about a time when you solved a problem." This calls for a specific example of when the candidate solved a particular problem.

Why Behavioral Interviewing?

Research conducted over the last three decades indicates that in situations in which only traditional interview questions are asked, up to 75 percent of the people hired do not meet performance expectations once they start the job. Some candidates interview well, but when it comes to performance, they aren't what they claimed to be. According to *BusinessWeek*, companies that adopted behavioral interviewing techniques in the interviewing and hiring process claim to make better hiring decisions and have as much as five times better success with retention and performance than they were using the traditional interviewing style. Because of costly hiring mistakes, employers have become more cautious about hiring on the basis of "gut feelings."

When you use behavioral interviewing techniques to draw out specific examples of a job candidate's past behavior, you can determine more accurately the candidate's ability to perform under similar circumstances. In other words, what past behavior can this person bring to this company—what successes will be repeated in this job? Can this person save the company time, money, or work effort?

The more recent and similar the example to the job you are attempting to fill, the better the information you will have to make a decision about this candidate.

Sample Behavioral Questions

Behavioral questions *always* asks for a specific incident. Following are ways to lead into such questions:

- Tell me about a time when . . .
- Can you give me an example?
- Describe a situation . . .
- Describe a time when . . .
- Recall a time that . . .

Each question will ask for a time or an example. An example of a behavioral question would be, "Tell me about a time when you had to deal with a disgruntled customer."

If the answer given is not an example of a specific incident in which the candidate had to deal with a customer who was angry, the candidate will not have answered the question. Because you did not get what you wanted from the question, you will need to ask follow-up questions to get the answer.

Some candidates will not be able to provide you with a specific example. They either won't be able to think of an example, or perhaps they haven't had the experience that they claim they have. It will take some persistence or judgment on your part to determine if the person is just talking or whether he or she does have the specific skills it takes to do the job. In order to assess an accurate pattern of a candidate's true behavior, you will need to hear specific examples.

Spin Me a Tale

When you ask situational or "what if" questions, candidates can make up any answer. In other words they can "spin you a tale." An example of a situational question would be, "What would you do if you had to deal with a disgruntled customer?"

You can see how this question differs from the behavioral question because it does not ask for an example. The object of the situational question is to determine how the candidate thinks.

When you ask "what if" questions, you will want to listen to hear the thought process of the candidates. Listen carefully to determine how they "think on their feet" or how they go about solving a problem.

Probing for Specific Examples

Before you give up on candidates who cannot answer a behavioral question, there is a technique that you can use to try to help them through the example. That technique is called "probing," or digging deeper. If candidates do not give you an example the first time, you will want to help them through the example with some probes.

Here are some examples of probes that will help you get the rest of the story:

- What was your role in that project?

- When you say "we," what part of "we" was you?

- How did that work out in the end?

- Could you be more specific with the steps you took?

- What did you mean by that statement?
- When was the last time that happened?
- Would you handle it differently knowing what you know now?

Compare and Contrast

Another way to dig deeper into the answer is to ask the candidate to "compare and contrast" one job with another. This exercise will help you determine the fit of the candidate to your situation.

To determine fit, one successful technique is to look back at past behavior and experiences. When has the candidate been most satisfied in his or her career? When has the candidate been most dissatisfied?

By asking these questions and asking the candidates to compare and contrast their answer against your job opening, you may uncover information that might otherwise not have been uncovered. Many candidates haven't thought through the satisfaction they achieved in a particular job; they are just intent on getting the job.

Behavioral Patterns—Red Lights

Sometimes you can be so impressed with the appearance and demeanor of the person you are interviewing that you fail to see the "red lights" flashing. The red lights are indicators that this person has had problems with performance or behavior in previous positions or that this person is looking for a job just to have a job with no real interest in the position or the company. Chances are this person will soon leave your company if something better comes along.

For example, if a person has had short spans of employment over the last five or so years, there could be a logical reason for this, such as layoffs with certain industries being hit hard because of economic trends and outsourcing. On the other hand, the problem could be deeper. It will be your job to probe deeper to discover the real reason for the behavior.

There are many reasons why people change companies, and not all are bad reasons.

It will be your job to turn up your listening skills and to read between the lines to determine whether this person has a problem or has been able to roll with changes in industries and good and bad economies.

As you can see, after reading this chapter, there is more to interviewing than asking questions and getting answers. The challenge for you as the interviewer is what to do with the information you get in an answer. If you are a savvy interviewer, you will know what you expect in a candidate and you will take the information and analyze what you have heard based on your requirements list. Where is the candidate a strong fit? And where are areas for improvement, or is further experience needed? Were you impressed enough with this candidate to make allowances for the areas that require skills that can be taught?

Step Three
Interview Structure and Techniques

Opening the Interview: Getting to Know the Candidate

From the first handshake, the interview has officially begun, and what is said from this point forward is considered part of the interview. Judgments will be made by both parties.

It is your job as the interviewer to be the host and to treat the candidate as your guest. You can do this in a number of ways, but the words you use will indicate your sincerity to make your guest feel welcome.

Chances are the candidate you are about to interview will be nervous when you first meet. In order to put the candidate at ease, it would be beneficial for both of you to make some small talk before the formal questioning begins. Although this sounds simple enough, for some people it is an unfamiliar and painful task.

Surprisingly, in our world of advanced technology, our communication skills have become less effective. People are losing their ability to talk to each other, especially making "small talk with someone they don't know."

Here are some examples of how you can use small talk in an interview to set the candidate at ease. Note that these suggestions make use of open-ended questions:

- "What was traffic like coming across the bridge?"
- "How is your summer going so far?"
- "This weather is something else, isn't it? Which do you prefer—hot or cold weather?"
- "What was your trip like?"

141

Small talk should be low key and general. Try not to ask questions that can be answered with one word such as yes or no.

The ice-breaking session should last for a couple of minutes and should always remain at a professional level. You should not discuss anything that is controversial or in any way discriminatory or derogatory.

If you turn up your listening and observation skills, you will find that even while you chat informally, you will be able to pick up clues as to the person's preferred method of doing things. While the goal of the small talk is to put the candidate at ease, it is still a part of the interview process, particularly if you are judging a candidate on social or interpersonal skills.

Encourage and Reassure the Candidate
The careful interviewer is aware of key rules and regulations and avoids making snap judgments by stereotyping rather than selecting the candidate based on his or her qualifications for the job. Encouraging the candidate will help you see the real person and to get information you might not otherwise have gotten. The following are general tips and information to think about *before* the interview:

- Smile and attempt to put the candidate at ease at the beginning of the interview. Establishing rapport with the candidate is essential for a successful interview.

- Be completely passive, no matter what you hear. Sometimes candidates want to share inappropriate information during the interview. This is not the time to judge or give advice. Try to listen without changing your expression.

- Use restatements or reflections. Good listening skills include a technique that demonstrates that you heard what the person said by reflecting back comments. An example is, "It sounds like you had a difficult time in that position."

- Use varied posture to indicate interest and animation. Nonverbal clues are just as important as verbal clues. If candidates think you are not paying attention by your posture, they may shut down. Leaning forward or shifting in your chair helps keep you focused on the candidates and what they're saying.

- Use good vocal expression and energy. Just as you pick up or lose energy from the candidate, he or she in turn will reflect your style through your vocal tone and expressions.

- Encourage candidates by head nodding and "uh-huh" statements. Nodding your head occasionally is a signal to the applicant that you are listening and that he or she is on the right track.

While it is important for you to encourage candidates and reassure them that they are doing a good job, there are also some pitfalls to be aware of. The following story illustrates this:

Helen was the type of person who went out of her way to encourage the candidates she interviewed to help them feel confident that they were doing a good job.

In one particular interview she told the woman that she really enjoyed talking with her and that she had done a great job of interviewing. The woman told her that she also had enjoyed the interview and really looked forward to working with her. Helen smiled and wished her good luck.

Unfortunately, the woman was not hired. When the woman received the rejection letter from Helen telling her that the company had hired someone who was a better fit for the position, she became very upset.

Some days later Helen was called into HR to defend herself against an allegation that this woman was making. The woman claimed that Helen had all but promised her the job, and she was now protesting her rejection. Helen was shocked. She had not meant to imply in any way that the woman would be hired, but that this is what the woman interpreted from her praise.

When interviewing a person you do not know, it is always best to be on the conservative side with comments that might be misinterpreted. Be sure to explain that other candidates are being interviewed and that everyone will be rated on his or her experience and fit for the job.

> This process is not about people "liking" you; it's about your finding the right person for the job.

Begin Broad and Move to Specific

After a few minutes of small talk, it's time to start asking candidates questions about their experience. The best way to start this part of the interview process is with broad or open-ended questions. These are questions that can be used for any position. Examples of broad or open-ended questions are:

- Tell me about yourself.

- How would you describe yourself?

- What are three words that describe you?

You are attempting to get information to use as a springboard to then move to more specific questions. In other words, the things you hear in the answers to these questions will supply you with more focused or specific questions to ask. Here are some specific questions that might result from something you picked up in the answer to a general question:

- Could you tell me more about the project you mentioned from your last position?

- I'd like to hear more about the 20 percent saving you achieved at your last company.

- Can you give an example of a time when you used those excellent problem-solving skills you mentioned?

When candidates mention something in the interview or have written it on their résumé, that information becomes fair game for you to ask questions about. If, for instance, candidates say they are very organized, you can probe to find out what being very organized means to them. Ask for a specific project or time when their organizational skills made a difference. This would be a behavioral question: Can you tell me about a time when you were able to make a difference in a project because of your organizational skills?

The answer to this question will tell you whether candidates are using interview jargon or whether they really have the "very organized" skills they claim to have.

The Structured Interview

Interviews and interviewers come in all shapes and sizes. There is no set standard for interviewing, and so you may conduct interviews according to your own or your company's standards. It will be in your best interest to have some structure to your interview, even if your general discussion is unstructured.

If you work for a large corporation, chances are the HR department has taken care of the forms and sometimes even the coordinating of the interview. An interview in a corporation or large organization tends to be more structured, meaning each candidate is asked the same questions.

The Unstructured Conversation

If you are working for a smaller company, it may be up to you to set up and coordinate some type of order or system to evaluate job candidates in a fair and impartial manner.

Unstructured interviews or informal questions are like a conversation and can flow from one subject to another with no particular pattern. The setting can also be flexible and can be as informal as a bench in a mall or a room in a hotel. No two interviews are alike. There may not be forms or a rating system.

If you decide to use the unstructured interview, think about the factors you are looking for in this person. That way you will have some level of objectivity regarding your choice based on facts rather than a gut feeling.

Note Taking during the Interview

You should take notes so that you will be able to recall what the candidate said when you are comparing candidates and rating the interview. Use judgment with note taking, making sure that your note writing isn't taking over the process or hampering your ability to connect with the candidate.

Remember, it is challenging to give your full attention to someone while you're taking copious notes. The key word here is *moderation*. Avoid being so busy taking notes that you cannot observe the candidate, thereby missing out on body language, eye contact, and general demeanor.

Team and Panel Interviewing

Team or panel interviewing takes a great deal of coordination. If your company has an HR department, it will often coordinate the logistics of the interviews and provide each interviewer with a copy of the résumé or other documents needed.

If you are the coordinator of the interview and it is to be a panel interview, you will need to prepare questions and then provide each member of the panel with the questions along with a copy of the résumé or any other information that they will need.

The usual practice in a panel or group interview is for each panel member to ask a different question so that the other members of the panel can observe and take notes.

After the interview it will be necessary to somehow coordinate the information and get a consensus, either through a meeting or through a central person who becomes the coordinator.

It will be easier for everyone concerned if one person handles the ratings and coordinates any follow-up discussion, particularly when there is a disagreement about whether to make this person an offer or not.

The Close

In a competitive job market where the best candidates are being courted, the interviewer will have to work at selling the company; its reputation, mission, stability, and general benefits. Whether the HR department takes care of this part of the interview or whether it is up to you, the candidate should leave the interview with a sales pitch about the company, the position, and the good reasons for working at your company.

You will want to discuss your company's philosophy or mission statement. Candidates will also be interested in what makes your company special or unique. Assuming that they have done due diligence ahead of the interview, they will now be interested in the internal information about the department, team, or company.

"Do You Have Any Questions?"

At some point in the interview you will want to elicit questions from the candidate. Some hiring managers think that what the candidate asks or doesn't ask can provide the most telling information.

For instance, if all candidates ask about are the vacation days and sick benefits, you could get the idea that their interest is in time away from the job. This could be a possible red flag.

Listen for intelligent questions that are about the company or job, specifically. If there is no interest in the company or what you have been talking about, maybe this person does not feel especially energized by the idea of working at your company. He or she may not be the right person for the job.

Handling Difficult Questions and Situations

For a variety of reasons there may be times when you will have to handle difficult questions about the job or your company. It is best to be as honest as you can be, yet diplomatic. A good rule to follow is to never become emotional about anything said during an interview. Even if you don't agree with or are offended by what a candidate says, stay calm and end the interview as quickly as possible without being rude to the candidate.

When handling difficult situations, make sure you stay in control and calm. As an extreme example, if the candidate were to become ill during the interview, call for the appropriate help immediately. Another example would be if there was a security issue to deal with. Again, stay in control and call for the proper assistance.

Explaining the Job and the Responsibilities

While the job description gives the candidate general information about the job, it will be your responsibility to fill in the blanks. The candidate will want to know information about the job responsibilities and the kind of interaction he or she will be expected to have with others. Candidates should leave the interview with a very good picture of what will be expected of them in this job. Only then can they evaluate if the job is the right job for them.

You should be prepared to talk about the position and the company and to respond to any questions the candidate has. If you do not have the answers to the questions, then take notes and promise that you will find out. Be sure if you promise to do something that you do as promised. This could be a reflection on the company and how the candidate can expect to be treated if hired. It could leave a positive or negative impression.

Your genuine enthusiasm during this period could convince the candidate or deter the candidate from accepting an offer.

Selling the Company and the Benefits

As the cost of health care and other benefits have soared, the benefits package your company offers has become more valuable and at the same time must be competitive with other companies trying to attract the best candidates. You will want to present some kind of information packet outlining your benefits program. If you are a small company, a simple folder and copies of information will suffice.

What's the Next Step?

Whether you are interviewing ten candidates or one candidate, each candidate will want to know the next step or part of the process that will take place leading to the decision. If you have a deadline for a decision, you should share it with the candidate.

The deadline will depend on whether you are the sole interviewer or whether others are involved in the decision. Either way, there should be some plan in place before bringing people in to interview. Some companies lose valuable candidates by dragging out the process because of a lack of a plan.

Follow Through on a Promise

A cardinal rule in interviewing should be, "If you say you're going to do something, *do it!*" One of the most inconsiderate things you can do as an interviewer it to promise to call the candidate and then not follow through as promised.

For you this promise may not mean a great deal, but to the candidate waiting by the phone to hear whether he or she got the job it means a great deal. Not only is it inconsiderate to have taken an hour or more of the person's time; but it is rude not to give him or her the courtesy of a call, an e-mail, or at least a form letter. Many companies don't feel that it is necessary to have anything to do with job candidates once they have been rejected. Wrong!

This could fall under the heading of good common sense. But the truth is that some interviewers are "bad" interviewers. The candidates come away from the interview feeling that the person interviewing them didn't give them a fair chance at proving themselves. They feel that they were treated rudely or that the person doing the interviewing didn't really know what he or she was looking for or what to do with the information that they provided.

Surely you do not want to fall into this category of being a bad interviewer. All candidates should be treated as though they are an important guest. Any promises made should be followed through on. And you should keep the candidate posted as to the progress of the interview if you fail to meet your prescheduled deadline.

Remember that the person you interview will go to another company sooner or later and will remember your company through the way that you conducted your interview and the courtesy you extended. In fact, some candidates have been know to hire good people away from companies where they were treated shabbily because they had a pretty good idea that this treatment was the way that the employees were treated once they were hired.

Time spent being cordial and courteous could make a difference to your company's reputation and ultimately affect your employee retention rate.

The Candidate Evaluation

Evaluating and Rating the Candidate

Here is another familiar scenario:

The door opens and Brian sees his interviewer appear across the lobby—eye contact is made for the first time. He immediately tenses and begins to sweat. His heart rate begins to increase. He can feel his hands getting moist. It's a feeling he's had before—interview anxiety!

He begins to thinks negative thoughts, "I can't do this. I won't know the answers. I'm going to look like a fool. Everybody else is going to do better than I am in the interview. I will be rejected again."

By the time the interviewer has crossed the lobby and extended her hand, Brian is having meltdown and doesn't even remember to give a good firm handshake and smile. He has failed before he has even opened his mouth to speak, and he has done it to himself!

Although it may be a challenge, be aware of prejudices and opinions you've formed from previous experiences. This will pay off when you're making a final decision about a candidate.

Sometimes candidates can look as though they are perfect for the job until you begin to question behaviors—past and present. You may find that there is a lack of experience or substance once you dig below the surface.

On the other hand, candidates who make a poor first impression may be diamonds in the rough. But you can find this out only if you take the time to listen and probe to find out about these people and their experiences.

Nonverbal Clues

There is no doubt that people's attire, posture, and grooming can affect how we judge them. People who do not wear the proper attire to an interview may be sending a clear message that this is who they are and that they don't necessarily want to change. This could be a possible red flag.

Eye contact, or lack of it, can be a giveaway about people's self-confidence. Watch candidates' eyes for clues to their comfort level, especially when they're talking about themselves. Also, keep in mind that there are certain cultures that have a problem with eye contact; so before you jump to conclusions, stop and to consider why candidates may be doing what they're doing.

Communication Style and Confidence

Besides eye contact, posture, and demeanor there will be other clues as to whether candidates you are interviewing are confident and sure of themselves.

Communication style will vary according to the level of responsibility that you are interviewing for. You would expect someone applying for a management position to have a strong command of language and vocabulary. When interviewing for a mailroom or warehouse job, however, vocabulary and language skills may not be as important, although good communication skills will always be necessary if a person is to interact with other people.

It is a good rule of thumb to think of this person as a possible representative of your company, a person you could be proud to send to interact with your most prestigious customer.

Patterns and Words

A sign of an accomplished interviewer is someone who can listen and hear what is *not being* said as well as what *is being* said. By listening and reading between the lines, you will find that you are able to ask questions and bring out information that would otherwise not be heard. The following story illustrates this perfectly:

> *Michael was interviewing for a job as an HR coordinator. During the interview he gave an example of quitting a basketball team earlier in his life because he had life conflicts and it became too difficult to handle everything at once.*
>
> *When asked why he had left some of his other jobs, he talked about finding the work to be dull and not as much fun as in the beginning. He also talked about quitting his pursuit of a degree because he decided putting his effort into his career was more important.*

The interviewer began to see a pattern of someone who quits when the going gets tough. Because this position required someone to rise above adversity, there was a concern that Michael would not be able to hang in when things were tense or stressful.

Listening is one of the most important skills that an interviewer can develop. Listening and looking for certain words or patterns will weed out the poor candidates and assist you in finding the candidates who are a good fit for your job.

The most convincing answers to your questions will be those that are examples of past experiences. When you can get specific examples of performance in similar situations, you will be able to compare whether this person can do the job. Remember, if this person did it before, he or she can do it again.

These examples include any results they've achieved as well as failures. It is not the example itself that will tell the story, but the skills and traits you will hear about as you listen to the story.

Train yourself to note certain qualities you hear as the example or story is being presented. Some examples of skills or traits that you could hear in a story are, "took the initiative," "good interpersonal skills," "a team player—good people interaction ," "good problem-solving skills."

When listening to specific examples, keep in mind that you are listening for comparisons with the job that you have open so that you will be able to determine whether this person has the skills and experiences necessary to perform in your position.

Consensus/Comparison Rating

The rating system you use will depend on the circumstances and number of people who will be interviewing the candidate. If you are the only person doing the interviewing, the decision of whom to hire rests with your rating system alone.

When you have multiple interviewers, there will be multiple opinions. Because each person will have his or her own agenda, there is bound to be differences as to whether this is the right person for the job or not. By using an objective rating system, you can take some of the subjectivity out of the process and resolve some of the disagreements that can occur when a candidate is being rated.

There will most likely be built-in prejudices and doubts based on past experiences on the part of some of the team members. If you are the appointed coordinator, listen and hear each person out. One way to make the process more objective is to assign a weight or percentage to the relative importance or value of certain tasks. These can be of value in breaking a tie or when there's a difference of opinion.

For example, if a team member does not think the candidate has strong enough analytical problem-solving skills, assign a percentage to analytical problem solving. Let's say it equates with 50 percent of job success. Since this is a high percentage, this perceived flaw should be discussed until everyone agrees whether or not this could be a problem that could affect this person's ability to perform on this job.

Rating the Candidates against One Another

You have come to the point at which you have rated each candidate, and you must now rate the candidates against one another, assuming you have more than one candidate who appears to be a good fit for the job.

You will want to ask two basic questions:

1. Can he do the job?

2. Do we like her—will she fit in?

Can He Do the Job?

Because you've established the hiring criteria at the very beginning of this process, you know the requirements and the qualifications that you are seeking.

Below is an example of an exercise that can assist you in bringing more objectivity to the hiring process. Of course, the final decision is always somewhat subjective, but this allows you to compare and contrast the criteria and the qualifications of each candidate.

ANSWERS

List each requirement or qualification on the left hand side of a sheet of paper. Next write the name of each candidate that you are considering across the top of the page (writing it diagonally works best).

If you have decided to use a weight or a percentage as a deciding factor, then add that after each qualification on your rating sheet.

You will now rate each candidate for each requirement. After you've completed the exercise, total the columns and see whether someone has significantly more points that the others.

	Jim Brown	Jane Smith	Bill Jones	Mary Martin
Past experience a good fit (35%)	5	5	5	5
Analytical ability (10%)	5	3	4	5
Communication/people skills (25%)	2	5	4	2
Detail/multitasking ability (10%)	3	5	3	2
Attention to detail (10%)	3	5	5	3
Good attitude (10%)	2	5	4	2
Final rating	20	28	25	19

Notice that all candidates are rated equally when it comes to past experience (weighted at 35 percent). That will often be the case if you have screened the résumés you've received well and invited only qualified candidates to interview.

The next category rates their analytical ability (weighted at 10 percent) and the ratings become more varied. Ratings for communication/people skills (weighted at 25 percent) vary dramatically with two of the higher analytical achievers rating much lower in this category.

Detail/multitasking ability ratings (weighted at 10 percent) also have a large margin of difference. Two candidates are more proficient in the area of attention to detail (weighted at 10 percent). Good attitude (weighted at 10 percent) is a subjective rating based on the performance or the tone detected during the interview.

It is clear that Jane Smith has the highest score in the rating system. She also has rated highest in the areas that are weighted most heavily—experience, communication/people skills, detail/multitasking, and attention to detail. She did, however, rate the lowest in analytical ability.

Bill Jones is right behind Jane in his score and has rated higher in the analytical ability category, but he has rated lower in the area of communication/people skills, detail/multitasking, and attitude.

Jim Brown has also rated high in the areas of experience and analytical ability but lower in all the other categories. Last in the running is Mary Martin, who has scored high marks only in the areas of experience and analytical ability.

Do We Like Her—Will She Fit In?

With the scores being somewhat close, the next part of the decision-making process becomes more subjective as you look at what's important to the job and the team of people that this person will be working with.

The more subjective categories of interpersonal skills—communication/people skills and good attitude—will make or break the decision here.

Once again, if you are the only interviewer, you will make a decision based on your own findings—objective or subjective—but the rating system may assist you with a difficult decision .

If you are working with a team of people in this process, you will have to decide if the scores alone will be the determining factor. If everyone does this exercise and comes up with similar numbers, this should tell you something about the effectiveness of your rating system and whether you want to continue using it.

Although the system may not be perfect, it is more objective than rating candidates on their appearance and demeanor.

Misrepresented Qualifications

Rarely you may find out that someone is misrepresenting his or her qualifications. You can get back in touch with the candidate to continue a line of questioning if you have doubts, but it would be unwise to accuse someone of falsifying credentials or qualifications during the interview.

After the interview, check out your suspicions by calling a former employer or learning institution for verification. If you find that there is a misrepresentation, you will know that this is not the person for the position.

If you have an application for the candidate to fill out, there is usually a statement at the end that says in some manner, "Misrepresentation of qualifications can be subject to dismissal." It is far easier to check credentials and not hire the person than it is to go through the embarrassment of a confrontation and having to fire people because you found out that they had lied on the application or during the interview.

When It's Clear the Candidate Isn't Right

During the interview, if it becomes clear that candidates aren't right for your position, you have to make a judgment as to how to finish the interview. You have several choices:

- You can stop the interview by telling the candidates that rather than go further, you can see that this position is not a good fit on whatever grounds you find. An example is if a candidate does not have the technical knowledge necessary to perform the job.

- You can give candidates the courtesy of going through the basics of the interview, giving them an opportunity to present themselves.

- You can go through the entire interview process with the hope that you can discover if candidates could be a good fit for another position within your company.

- You can check in with the candidates and ask if this is the position that they had in mind when they applied for the job, because there seems to be some mismatch of qualifications and needs. Listen to the candidates' answer to decide whether to go on or end the interview now.

No matter what happens in the interview, it is important that candidates not feel like they have been in a hostile situation. Candidates have taken the trouble to travel to your company, or specified location, because they have an interest in a position that you have advertised in one way or another. Candidates have also taken time from their day, and perhaps even time off from another job, to interview with you.

It is your responsibility to treat candidates as if they are a guest in your workplace. They should be treated with respect and courtesy and never treated as though they are inferior.

They also deserve the courtesy of a follow-up, whether it be through an e-mail, a letter, or a phone call, thanking them for taking the time to talk with you, regardless of whether or not a job offer is made.

Think of yourself as an ambassador of your company, someone who can make a difference in the reputation of that company. The world has become a small place, and one never knows what situation you will be in from day to day. The person you interview and treat badly may have the opportunity to be your interviewer some day. You just never know.

Appendix
Five Rules to Improve Your Hiring Process

1. **Assess the job before the interview. What is the role of the job?**

   - Talk to the person leaving the job to find out what the job entails.
   - Ask how the job could be done more efficiently—adding/deleting tasks.
   - Talk with customers (internal and external) and end users to assess their needs.

2. **Identify the job's "key factors" for success.**

   - What knowledge-based experience is needed to do this job? (Example, education)
   - What transferable skills are necessary to succeed? (Example, communication)
   - What personality traits will be needed to do this job? (Example, friendly)

3. **Prepare questions to ask during the interview.**

   - Prepare questions based on identified "key factors."
   - Include questions that ask for examples of past behavior in previous jobs.
   - Prepare a list of secondary questions to probe deeper.

4. **Include all interviewers in the plan/process.**

    - Provide each interviewer with a list of "key factors."

    - Make a list of suggested questions for each interviewer.

    - Each interviewer should cover a specific area of concern.

5. **Objectively review the results and rate the candidate after the interview.**

    - Collect input from each interviewer.

    - Rate each candidate using the "key factors" (rating scale of 1–5).

    - Make a hiring decision based on consensus feedback.

Index

About the Author

Carole Martin is a professional interviewer, coach, and an expert on the subject of interviewing. As an interview coach she coaches both candidates and interviewers on the fine art of interviewing and making savvy selections.

In addition to having her own business, she has been an interview expert and a contributing writer for Monster.com for over five years. Her articles appear on countless Internet sites.

Carole's unique background includes over 18 years of Human Resources Management experience (SPHR). She has worked in technical and non-technical industries, in Fortune 500 companies, as well as for start-up companies.

Her education includes a master's degree in Career Development from John F. Kennedy University in Pleasant Hill, California, where she currently is an adjunct faculty member teaching interviewing techniques to future counselors. Her undergraduate degree is in Communications and Public Relations from San Jose State University (achieved at age 40). She has been certified as a Senior Professional in Human Resources (SPHR) by The Human Resources Certification Institute, and has received training at the Coaches Training Institute. She is a certified "Behavioral Interviewer."

Carole has been recognized as an interview expert on several TV shows (CNN-FN, New York Viewpoint, San Diego, and Sacramento shows). She has been a guest on numerous radio shows, including four shows in Canada and the BBC. She is quoted frequently in newspapers and magazines—*New York Times, LA Times; Men's Health, HR Magazine, Smart Money, Parents* magazine, *Employment Management Today, Details, Wall Street Journal.com, Employment Review, Self* magazine, *RT Image*, and *Marie Claire* magazine.

She has authored three books on job search and interviewing: *Interview Fitness Training; Boost Your Interview IQ*, which was voted one of the Top Career Books of 2004; and *Perfect Phrases for the Perfect Interview*. She is a frequent speaker and presenter to groups of both job seekers and HR professionals. Her Web sites are www.interviewcoach.com and www.HRcoachingclub.com.